CRITICAL PERSPECTIVES ON RURAL CHANGE

Volume 6

GENDER AND RURALITY

I0094058

GENDER AND RURALITY

Edited by
SARAH WHATMORE,
TERRY MARSDEN
AND
PHILIP LOWE

Routledge
Taylor & Francis Group

LONDON AND NEW YORK

First published in 1994 by David Fulton Publishers Ltd.

This edition first published in 2023
by Routledge
4 Park Square, Milton Park, Abingdon, Oxon OX14 4RN

and by Routledge
605 Third Avenue, New York, NY 10158

Routledge is an imprint of the Taylor & Francis Group, an informa business

© 1994 David Fulton Publishers Ltd

All rights reserved. No part of this book may be reprinted or reproduced or utilised in any form or by any electronic, mechanical, or other means, now known or hereafter invented, including photocopying and recording, or in any information storage or retrieval system, without permission in writing from the publishers.

Trademark notice: Product or corporate names may be trademarks or registered trademarks, and are used only for identification and explanation without intent to infringe.

British Library Cataloguing in Publication Data
A catalogue record for this book is available from the British Library

ISBN: 978-1-032-49781-5 (Set)
ISBN: 978-1-032-49762-4 (Volume 6) (hbk)
ISBN: 978-1-032-49779-2 (Volume 6) (pbk)
ISBN: 978-1-003-39538-6 (Volume 6) (ebk)

DOI: 10.4324/9781003395386

Publisher's Note
The publisher has gone to great lengths to ensure the quality of this reprint but points out that some imperfections in the original copies may be apparent.

Disclaimer
The publisher has made every effort to trace copyright holders and would welcome correspondence from those they have been unable to trace.

CRITICAL PERSPECTIVES
ON
RURAL CHANGE SERIES

GENDER AND RURALITY

EDITED BY

SARAH WHATMORE
TERRY MARSDEN
PHILIP LOWE

David Fulton Publishers
London

David Fulton Publishers Ltd
2 Barbon Close, London WC1N 3JX

First published in Great Britain by
David Fulton Publishers 1994

Note: The right of the authors to be identified as the authors of this work has been
asserted by them in accordance with the Copyright, Designs and Patents Act 1988.

Copyright © David Fulton Publishers Limited

British Library Cataloguing in Publication Data

A catalogue record for this book is available from the British Library

ISBN 1-85346-252-7

All rights reserved. No part of this publication may be reproduced, stored in a
retrieval system or transmitted, in any form, or by any means, electronic,
mechanical, photocopying, recording or otherwise, without the prior permission of
the publishers.

Typeset by Franklin Graphics, Formby
Printed and bound in Great Britain by
Biddles Ltd, Guildford and King's Lynn

Contents

Contributors

Agnes Bolsø   Centre for Rural Research
                     University of Trondheim
                     Norway

Berit Brandth   Centre for Rural Research
                     University of Trondheim
                     Norway

Marit S. Haugen   Centre for Rural Research
                     University of Trondheim
                     Norway

Jo Little   Faculty of the Built Environment
                     University of the West of England
                     Bristol
                     UK

Linda M. Lobao   Department of Agricultural Economics and Rural
                     Sociology
                     Ohio State University
                     Columbus, Ohio
                     USA

Philip Lowe   Centre for Rural Economy
University of Newcastle
UK

Terry Marsden   School of Geography and Earth Resources
University of Hull
UK

Katherine Meyer   Department of Sociology
Ohio State University
Columbus, Ohio
USA

Patricia O'Hara   Callaghan Associates
Dublin, Eire

Carolyn Sachs   Dept. of Agricultural Economics and Rural
Sociology
Pennsylvania State University
USA

Mathilde Schmitt   Department of Sociology
University of Essen
Germany

Elizabeth Teather   Department of Geography and Planning
University of New England
Armidale
Australia

Sarah Whatmore   Department of Geography
University of Bristol
UK

SERIES PREFACE

Critical Perspectives on Rural Change Series

This series aims to promote the international dissemination and debate of current empirical and theoretical research relevant to rural areas in advanced societies. Rural areas, their residents and agencies face considerable change and uncertainty. The balance between production, consumption and conservation is being adjusted as economic activities are relocated and primary production is transformed. Similarly the values placed upon rural living and landscape are altering. Local and external political forces structure choices within rural areas, not only for those concerned with agriculture, but also with regard to rural development, general economic and social policy, and regional fiscal arrangements. To understand contemporary rural change, therefore, demands a critical and holistic perspective able to transcend traditional disciplinary boundaries and to encompass different spatial and institutional levels of analysis. The series is intended to contribute to the development of such a perspective, and the volumes are designed to attract a wide audience associated with international comparative research. Each provides a review of current research within its subject.

Terry Marsden
Philip Lowe
Sarah Whatmore

INTRODUCTION

Feminist Perspectives in Rural Studies

Sarah Whatmore, Terry Marsden and Philip Lowe

Over the past decade, rural studies has seen a growth of research interest in rural women and particularly, the position of women within family farming (see, for example, special issues of key journals including the *Rural Sociologist,* 1981; *Sociologia Ruralis,* 1988; *Journal of Rural Studies,* 1991). Such a body of work clearly marks a significant improvement in the position of women on the rural research agenda but, has tended to be isolated as a discrete field of interest to the extent that at the beginning of the 1990s it could still be described as a 'fugitive literature' (Friedland, 1991: 315). The danger of the marginalisation of gender issues is undiminished, at least in the advanced industrial countries with which this series is concerned. Here, the significance of gender relations in the social and economic dynamics of rural life continues to be segregated as a specialism in which rural women and 'their' issues can be safely corraled by researchers and policy-makers, while mainstream research and policy concepts and concerns proceed untouched.

The papers comprising this volume were commissioned to illustrate a range of contemporary challenges to the established boundaries of gender research in rural studies. They represent important departures in the development of feminist research perspectives in this arena; extending the analysis of the gendered construction of rurality beyond the family farm; highlighting the contested and heterogeneous nature of 'rural' women's experience; and exploring a greater diversity of threads in feminist theories of gender as an axis of social power and identity. In so doing, the collection exposes and explores serious voids in the research agendas and theories of 'critical', as well as mainstream, analyses of rural restructuring.

These new research energies and directions have been influenced in part by the changing impetuses of social theory, particularly the impression of feminist

1

theory on the social sciences and its encounters with postmodernism (Nicholson, 1990). Evident here is a transition from thinking about gender in terms of men and women as fixed social categories, exhibiting behaviours which accord with established social norms (gender role theories) (Connell, 1987) to reflexive, or interpretative, theories of the unstable and fragmented meanings and practices attached to gendered subjects (gender identity theories) (Fraser, 1989). This conceptual shift is multi-faceted and in no sense uniform, nor have all its dimensions and formulations found expression in rural research. The embeddedness of rural social science within the discourses of agricultural policy, professional and grass-roots agendas, has given a distinctively practical imperative to theoretical projects, in ways which mark it off from the 'literary turn' that has been so influential in the development of feminist theory more broadly. This distinctiveness restricts the influence of feminist work in rural studies on the shape of 'mainstream' feminist thinking and reproduces the theoretical 'lag-effect' noted more generally about rural research (Buttel *et al.*, 1990). At the same time, it is also a considerable strength, moderating the tendency towards self–referential insularity characteristic of much recent feminist writing (Segal, 1991). Rural researchers' sustained commitment to engaging with women (and men) involved in non-academic (and non-feminist) organisations and discourses, articulating very different visions of gender and rurality, is well represented in this volume.

An equally significant influence on the development of gender analysis in rural studies has been the consequences of rural restructuring, agricultural diversification and the shifting cultural politics of the meaning of rurality itself which are manifest in everyday experience, popular consciousness, and policy and media discourses. These transformative processes are implicated in the destabilisation of postwar regimes of agricultural regulation in industrialised nation states and international institutions. The contours of any new regimes are still in the making and the subject of intense political energies within regional and national polities, as well as in the global realignment of food trade, technologies and institutional interests (McMichael, 1993). In this context, the traditional focus on farming in isolation has become increasingly problematic, as policy and research follow the experiences of people living on the land in recognising the growing hybridity of rural land-uses. This hybridity derives not just from the ties between farming and wider food complexes but from the increasingly diverse interweaving of agriculture, as a definitive rural land-use, with the commoditisation of rural social and environmental relations as consumption goods.

The interests contesting rural restructuring build on and, in turn, reshape gender relations; empowering and disempowering women (and men) in different ways in particular localities, complicated by their intersection with other axes of social power relations, notably class, 'race' and ethnicity. For example, a recent report to the European Commission's Equal Opportunities Unit (CE, 1991) records major shifts in rural women's work in southern Europe, from unpaid family labour concentrated on traditional crops such as vines, olives and citrus, to increased self-employment as farm managers in Italy and Portugal; casual or seasonal wage-work in Spain; full and part-time factory work in food processing; and as homeworkers in textile industries. The unevenness in women's experience of rurality, rooted in the political and discursive economy of particular places, emerges from this collection of papers as a central issue for researchers and policy-makers in comprehending the significance of gender relations for understanding the process and pattern of rural change.

In this introductory chapter we outline some key developments in the analysis of gender in rural studies as these both incorporate, and influence, feminist perspectives and theories of rurality; identify the main contributions of each paper to this endeavour and indicate some directions for future research which emerge from the issues and approaches to which they draw attention.

Voicing the other

Barely more than ten years ago women were all but invisible in research and policy accounts of the farming industry in advanced industrial countries as the concepts of work and the treatment of 'the family' continued to discount their presence and contribution. On a broader canvass, the isolation of the rural *labour* process as the sole, or dominant, focus of research interest eclipsed many dimensions of the social relations and cultural politics of rurality. This has created what Philo has termed a series of 'neglected rural geographies' (1992: 200) as those 'others', including women, whose lived experiences of rurality have been cast into the shadows by mainstream, and critical, analytical conventions. The concept of the rural labour process, for example, has tended to be confined to formal employment activities and to be measured against yardsticks which take the male worker and his work pattern as their norm, in such statistical units as the 'standard man day'. All the work which sustains households' labouring capacity on a daily basis, and contributes to household income and sustenance through informal and non-market relations – work traditionally performed by women – has been too readily overlooked (Gasson *et al.*, 1988).

'The family', on the other hand, which has characteristically been made much of in rural research as a distinctive feature of the social organisation of farming, and rural business and community relations more generally, has been treated as an organic entity accessed through, and represented by, a single individual – the farmer, or head of household, both masculine-defined terms (Delphy and Leonard, 1992). In this way the social divisions, power relations and inequalities within the family, household and labour relations sustaining rural social life have gone largely unrecognised. Equally significant, this unitary treatment has reinforced the ideological naturalisation of *the* family and its place in the moral economy of rurality and nation, effacing the socially constructed processes and relations of kinship and household (Strathern, 1992). Such naturalising ideologies of 'the family' inform the accounts of farming communities, policy-makers and researchers alike, and are directly related to the invisibility of women in these stories of rural life. They are inscribed, for example, in agricultural and social legislation in terms of women's treatment as dependents of a male head of household, compromising their rights as individuals to pension, unemployment and sickness provisions and their legal status in family businesses.

Research on women in farming was the first to begin the important task of trying to make women visible within the established categories and measures of labour and economic activity on the farm, in terms of hours worked, tasks performed and involvement in farm decision-making. This literature marks the most significant research transition in rural studies in the development of gender theory itself, moving away from questions about how to fit women in to a picture of farming implicitly defined by men's experiences and perspectives, as 'farmers', 'successors' and 'heads of households', to the task of redefining the basic terms and elements which are taken to describe farming and rural life in ways which admit women's experiences and perspectives as constitutive (see for example, Sachs, 1983; Whatmore, 1991; Fink, 1992).

At the risk of oversimplification, we can trace the passage of two main conceptual shifts in the treatment of gender in rural studies. The first centres on a transition from theories which take the categories of women and men as given, and by implication fixed, to those which see these categories as actively constructed through the meanings and practices which invest them with particular significance in everyday social interchange and are cemented into the institutional fabric of society in, for example, legal, medical and professional codes and protocols. The second, corrolary, shift centres on the recognition that the social categories 'women' and 'men' do not describe uniform experiences of femininity or masculinity but are cross-cut by other social divisions and identities, such as class and 'race', which are themselves socially constructed and dynamic.

These conceptual shifts intersect with attempts to rethink the nature of rurality as a distinctive configuration of socio-environmental relations and its currency as cultural capital in the formation and transformation of social identities. In seeking to better comprehend the interrelations between gender and rurality, the chapters in this volume begin to take up the concerns of those social theorists, most notably Michel Foucault and Anthony Giddens, consistently concerned with the spatial embeddedness of social life (Soja, 1989). Mormont (1990) and others have already begun to rethink the significance of the designation 'rural' along these lines, as socially constructed and dynamic, rather than geographically defined and fixed (see, particularly, Marsden et al., 1993). Understood in these terms, gender and rurality can be seen as unstable and interactive reference points in the constitution of dynamic and contested social identities, values and alliances. It follows that the meaningfulness of categories like 'rural' women (or men) becomes at once more problematic and more open to investigation in terms of the conditions and particularities of the intersection of rural and gender identities and practices. This intersection raises important questions about the overlaps between the discursive spaces of nationhood, rurality and domesticity in the mapping of historically specific moral and economic orders and the symbolic and substantive place of women within them (Davidoff et al., 1976; Davidoff and Hall, 1987; Armstrong, 1987).

These ideological processes are essential in understanding the dynamics of observable gender inequalities as a product of both coercion and consent, and in developing theories capable of accounting for the ways in which dominant identities and practices are not only sustained, but also challenged. Thus far in rural studies, such questions have begun to be addressed most fully in work on family farming. Such work uses a range of 'qualitative' research methods to investigate the everyday significance of what it means to be a women or a man for the ways in which those engaged in family farming make sense of, and legitimise, the power relations which structure their lives (for example Inhetveen, 1990; Thorsen, 1990). These methods place emphasis on allowing men and women to define their own work experience rather than fitting themselves into conventional or imposed categories, however awkward or distorting of that experience. Such methods are particularly important in giving a voice to women and, above all, to the multiplicity of diverse identities and activities which characterise their daily experience of the rural labour process.

These theoretical developments have shown that women enter and engage in farming through specific kinship relations, as wives, mothers and widows; their status determined primarily by what Pateman has called 'the sexual contract' (1988) which accords them little, if any, substantive stake in farm business or land assets. Men enter farming primarily through a structure of property inheritance organised by the male line which in practice, if not now in law, fashions sons rather than daughters as family 'successors' (Friedman, 1986). The construction of women as wives and men as farmers and successors is a social process undertaken, sometimes quite consciously, from the birth of children into farming families (see, particularly, Haugen in this volume). Additionally, such developments have advanced our understanding of the rural labour process, recasting the concept and analysis of economic activity to a more broadly defined domestic and 'informal economy', including homeworking, subsistence activities and casual or seasonal work, not just as fractions or sub-sets of full-time paid work, but as qualitatively different kinds of work experience and labour relation (Redclift and Mingione, 1985).

The extension of such insights, and the elaboration of new questions and perspectives, on the interweaving of the social constitution of gender and rurality beyond the particularities of farming remains an important challenge for feminist rural studies. At least three imperatives for breaking out of the analytical fencing around the family farm and exploring broader agendas are immediately apparent.

First, the diversification of farm livelihoods and their increasing interrelations with the wider rural economy, including off-farm waged work; para-agricultural farm enterprises such as tourism and food processing; homeworking and co-operative or community enterprises in producing and marketing 'new' environmental and artisanal products (Fitchen, 1991).

Second, the growing significance of the dynamics of the consumption of food and 'nature' as they become foci for the mobilisation of powerful social forces contesting rural land-use practices, whether centred on concerns about environmental sustainability, landscape protection, food safety, or nutrition and health (Kloppenburg, 1991).

Third, the cultural politics of rurality associated with a growing recognition of the persistent analytical and experiental forcefulness of the meaning and representation of the rural as these shape, and are shaped by, social struggles involving the (re)constitution of class, gender and national identities (Crouch, 1992).

It is under such imperatives that the papers in this volume begin to explore new directions and concerns in feminist rural studies. A number of consistent theoretical concerns and influences emerge from these papers, but they pursue disparate, and even in places, contradictory avenues of enquiry and lines of argument evading the regimentation of a single, or unified, approach.

The papers

The papers range in substantive focus across the gendered power relations of rural households and agricultural science, to farming unions and environmental protests. They are informed by different national contexts and local circumstances from the advanced capitalist world including the settler economies of the USA and Australia; the Scandinavian social democratic model of Norway; the colonially established industrial regimes of Germany and England and the late-industrialising European nation-state of Ireland. In disciplinary terms the dominant research traditions are those of geography and sociology. Against this background, the influence of feminist thinking on these contributions is, unsurprisingly, diverse. However, three main strands can be identified as being of sustained significance across more than one paper:

- feminist social geography concerned with the spatial embeddedness of gender relations (Chapters 1 and 2);
- feminist political theory concerned with the gendered construction of political agency and standing (Chapters 3, 4 and 5);
- feminist theories of science/knowledge, particularly as these articulate with alternative environmental thinking (Chapters 6, 7 and 8).

In the first chapter, Jo Little seeks to reconsider the rural restructuring process as it has been presented in critical research accounts by incorporating women's experiences of work as constitutive of the changing rural labour process. Based on original survey and interview data from different parts of England, her analysis shows the ways in which key elements in established accounts, rest on gendered assumptions about internal household relations and their articulation with the formal economy which are contradicted by women's experiences. Most importantly, her analysis challenges recent theories about the nature and significance of a new 'service class' in shaping the symbolic and substantive constitution of rurality.

Like this first chapter, the second contribution builds on, and informs, geographical theories of the spatial relations of rural change from a gender perspective. Elizabeth Teather examines the ways in which rurality, as a cultural and social construct, is deployed and reshaped in the political discourses and actions of rural women's organisations in Australia. Her central concern is with the interweaving of representations of feminine and rural identities in the literature and programmes of such organisations and the growing generational rift between 'traditionalist' and 'radical' constructions of rural womanhood.

In Chapter 3, Patricia O'Hara brings into focus a theme underlying many of the papers – the issue of power. Working with farm women in Ireland, she uses the results of in-depth interviews to elaborate a theoretical argument that power is best understood not as a rigid hierarchy of coercive oppression which leaves those in subordinate positions without the capacity to act, but as a *relational* process constituted through the active participation of all social agents in ways which accommodate and challenge prevailing hierarchies. She illustrates this argument with reference to the everyday exercise of authority and control by women in the patriarchal regimes of farming families and communities.

The next two chapters continue the concern with the constraints and capacities of rural women as political actors and agents of social change in rather different empirical contexts and fields of action. The fourth contribution by Katherine Meyer and Linda Lobao re-interrogates accounts of the US farm crisis from the perspectives of women in affected farming communities in the Midwest. They draw on feminist political theories to explore the modes of political organisation and consciousness *outside* the fabric of formal political institutions through which women voiced their experiences and responses to the farm crisis. The terms of women's political response were very different to those projected in the public discourses of the farming lobbies and policy agencies, which are dominated by men. Primarily, they argue, women experienced the farm crisis as a crisis of reproduction – rather than the officially documented crisis of production.

In Chapter 5, Marit Haugen examines the discrepancies between the formal equality of men and women in Norwegian property inheritance law and the gendered inequalities of farm succession in practice. Talking to parents and children involved in farm inheritance she reveals the limitations of the discourse and practice of 'equality', as the imposition of social standards and norms defined by the particular experiences and values of a relatively privileged group of white middle-class men. Her analysis makes clear that while such legislation is a necessary basis for formal justice, it fails to reflect or accord value to young women's experiences centred on a less individualistic sense of self. The disjuncture between legal and actual practice is related, she argues, to a gendered tension between ethical value systems which privilege individual rights and those which privilege social responsibility.

The last three chapters are, in different ways, coloured by the intersection of feminist theories of knowledge and science with ecofeminist concerns about the relationship between women and nature. In Chapter 6, Mathilde Schmitt brings an important body of ecofeminist thinking, associated the ideas and impacts of the German Greens, to the English-speaking research community for the first time. Germany has experienced the most rapid growth of organic and alternative agricultural land-use practices in Europe, strongly influenced by Green political mobilisation at national and state levels. The main theme of this contribution is to establish the significance of feminist-ecological thinking in this arena, and examine the role of the growing number of women farmers in Germany in translating such thinking into farming practice.

The seventh contribution by Carolyn Sachs picks up the significance of rural women's environmental activism in the US context. Drawing on the theoretical insights of Bina Agawal's conceptualisation of feminist environmentalism and Donna Haraway's interventions in feminist debates about science and the 'situatedness' of knowledge, she argues that rural women have particular understandings of environmental relations derived from their localities and everyday lives. This argument is grounded in an exploration of a range of environmental activist campaigns led by rural women around sustainable agriculture, forest conservation and toxic waste.

In the final chapter, Berit Brandth and Agnes Bolsø draw on the extensive feminist critique of science to re-examine debates about the ethical and health qualms surrounding the application of biotechnologies in agriculture and food production. Their primary concern is with the relationship between technology and gender in the field of agricultural science. Through a series of in-depth interviews with agricultural scientists, farmers and consumers in Norway, they examine the differences in men's and women's professional and personal responses to the ethical dilemmas raised by biotechnologies. Their analysis makes clear that the relationship between science and gender is far more complex than is assumed by essentialist expectations about differences in men's and women's values and relations with nature.

The papers in this volume cover a wide range of theoretical and empirical territory, reflecting the cultural and environmental diversity of rural areas in advanced capitalist societies. Between them they add further weight to the recognition in rural studies more widely, that theories of rural change need to be developed which build on, rather than eradicate, this diversity. It follows that one of the major theoretical challenges facing gender research is to incorporate this unevenness into conceptualisations of gender relations and identities and to recognise the highly differentiated nature of women's experiences of rural restructuring, associated with particular social and environmental contexts.

Women's access to, and control over, the rural labour process is likely to continue to revolve around two axes. Firstly, the double burden of combining so-called 'productive' work with domestic labour responsibilities, and secondly, legislative and actual changes in their individual rights to land and capital assets in family businesses and to state benefits and social security. Rural women's livelihoods are precariously balanced at the shifting intersection of a variety of disadvantaged forms of labour in agriculture and other rural industries; as unpaid family workers, casual and part-time waged workers and as homeworkers contracted to local firms. However, the constraints on, and opportunities for, securing improvements for rural women will vary regionally. Already younger rural women are challenging established inequalities in inheritance, autonomy and power by abandoning rural life and pursuing their aspirations in cities and towns.

In an intelligent consideration of what she calls critical theory's 'contemplative relation to the world', Joan Cocks (1989) argues that feminist 'theory must work not towards a celebration of . . . subordinate identit[ies] over the dominant but towards the subversion and explosion of both' (1989: 106). Such a vision highlights two major challenges for feminist rural studies in the future. First, having established that women fit poorly into the categories of work and economic activity which dominate policy discourses, more attention needs to be paid to the construction and dynamics of the dominant masculinities which define the social relations and discourses of rurality. A second challenge is to translate the feminist exposure of the many aspects of the social relations of rural areas which are eclipsed by current analytical conventions into a redefinition of the policy agenda. Without attention to these political and practical issues, the everyday assumptions and practices within the policy community, including advocacy organisations, will continue to ignore the significance of gender relations for the future viability of rural economies cultures and environments.

References

Armstrong, N. (1987) *Desire and Domestic Fiction. A Political History of the Novel.* Oxford University Press, Oxford.

Buttel, F., Larson, O. and Gillespie, G. (1990) *The Sociology of Agriculture.* Greenwood Press, Westport, Connecticut.

Cocks, J. (1989) *The Oppositional Imagination: Feminism, Critique and Political Theory.* Routledge, London.

Commission of the European Communities (1991) *Women of the South in European Integration: Problems and Prospects.* V/694/92–EN.

Connell, R. (1987) *Gender and Power.* Polity Press, Cambridge.

Crouch, D. (1992) Popular culture and what we make of the rural, with a case study of village allotments. *Journal of Rural Studies,* 8/3: 229–40.

Davidoff, L., L'Esperance, J. and Newby, H. (1976) Landscape with figures: home and community in English society. In Mitchel, J. and Oakley, A. (eds), *The Rights and Wrongs of Women*: 139–75. Penguin, Harmondsworth.

Davidoff, L. and Hall, C. (1987) *Family Fortunes. Men and Women in the English Middle Class 1780–1850.* Hutchinson, London.

Delphy, C. and Leonard, D. (1992) *Familiar Exploitation. A New Analysis of Marriage in Contemporary Societies.* Polity Press, Cambridge.

Fink, D. (1992) *Agrarian Women: Wives and Mothers in Rural Nebraska 1880–1940.* University of North Carolina Press, Chapel Hill.

Fitchen, J. (1991) *Endangered Spaces, Enduring Places: Change, Identity and Survival in Rural America.* Westview Press, Boulder, Colorado.

Fraser, N. (1989) *Unruly Practices. Power, Discourse and Gender in Contemporary Social Theory.* Minnesota University Press, Minneapolis.

Friedland, W. (1991) Women and agriculture in the United States: a state of the art assessment. In Friedland, W., Busch, L., Buttel, F. and Rudy, A.

(eds), *Towards a New Political Economy of Agriculture*: 315–38. Westview Press, Boulder, Colorado.

Friedmann, H. (1986) Property and patriarchy: a reply to Goodman and Redclift. *Sociologia Ruralis,* 26: 186–93.

Gasson, R., Crow, G., Errington, A., Hutson, J., Marsden, T. and Winter, M. (1988) The farm as a family business. *Journal of Agricultural Economics,* 39/1: 1–41.

Inhetveen, H. (1990) Biographical approaches to research on women farmers. *Sociologia Ruralis,* 30/1: 88–99.

Kloppenberg, J. (1991) Social theory and the de/reconstruction of agricultural science: local knowledge for an alternative agriculture. *Rural Sociology,* 56/4: 519–48.

Marsden, T., Murdoch, J., Lowe, P., Munton, R. and Flynn, A. (1993) *Constructing the Countryside.* UCL Press, London.

McMichael, P. (ed.) (1993) *Agro-food System Restructuring in the Late Twentieth Century: Comparative and Global Perspectives.* Cornell University Press, Ithaca, NY.

Mormont, M. (1990) Who is rural or, how to be rural? Towards a sociology of the rural. In Marsden, T., Lowe, P. and Whatmore, S. (eds), *Rural Restructuring: Global Processes and their Responses*: 21–44. David Fulton Publishers, London.

Nicholson, L. (1990) *Feminism/Postmodernism.* Routledge, London.

Pateman, C. (1988) *The Sexual Contract.* Polity Press, Cambridge.

Philo, C. (1992) Neglected rural geographies: a review. *Journal of Rural Studies,* 8/2: 193–207.

Redclift, N. and Mingione, E. (eds) (1985) *Beyond Employment: Household, Gender and Subsistence.* Blackwell, Oxford.

Sachs, C. (1983) *Invisible Farmers, Women's Work in Agricultural Production.* Rhinehart Allenheld, Totowa, NJ.

Segal, L. (1991) Feminism and the future. *New Left Review,* 185: 81–91.

Soja, E. (1989) *Postmodern Geographies: The Reassertion of Space in Critical Social Theory.* Verso, London.

Strathern, M. (1992) *After Nature. English Kinship in the Late Twentieth Century.* Cambridge University Press, Cambridge.

Thorsen, L. (1990) Espionage and the subjective. Reflections on life-course interviews as source material. *Ethnologia Scandinavica,* 20: 63–83.

Whatmore, S. (1991) *Farming Women: Gender, Work and Family Enterprise.* Macmillan, London.

CHAPTER 1

Gender Relations and the Rural Labour Process

Jo Little

Introduction

The restructuring literature provides, so Murdoch and Marsden (1991: 12) assert 'those concerned with rural change with a more accommodating . . . and flexible framework within which to study processes and outcomes'. Such literature has indeed included within it a number of radical attempts to redefine dominant social and economic divisions in rural areas and rethink established categories for the examination of rural change. In broad terms it has helped to locate the analysis of the rural economy and society in the context of international processes of capital accumulation. New boundaries and parameters have been introduced which allow 'the development of a broader conceptualisation of the rural problematic', and which see rural change within a global arena. At the same time, restructuring debates have reconfirmed the importance of locality in arguing that the characteristics of particular rural areas cannot be explained simply by reference to 'grand theory' and to the international circulation of capital. Rather they can only be understood in the analysis of a range of different social, economic, political and cultural relations interacting on a variety of spatial scales from the local through to the international.

The generation of new perspectives on rural change has both stemmed from, and contributed to, a recognition of the neglected significance of consumption, or more broadly, the process of reproduction (Redclift and Whatmore, 1990) in the evolution of rural spaces and populations. Work on the different forms of capitalist exploitation (see Marsden *et al.*, 1990) has drawn attention to the importance of property relations, and in particular access to and consumption

11

of housing, in the creation of social divisions in rural communities. Other research (for example Cloke and Thrift, 1990; Cloke, 1992) has demonstrated the existence of new 'fault lines' within traditional class groupings and linked the development of new class 'fractions' to consumption issues – above those surrounding rural property ownership.

Emerging from theoretical discussions of rural change within the 'restructuring debate' has been an acknowledgement of the unevenness of experience within individual households and a need for research (both theoretical and empirical) to focus specifically on the operation of social and economic relations at the household level (Redclift and Whatmore, 1990). The rural household as a subject of inquiry has received some attention – mainly from feminist researchers (see Delphy, 1984; Whatmore, 1991) who have drawn attention to the centrality of the household in the changing form of economic production and its relationship with the domestic division of labour. Such work has concentrated largely on the farm household and the theoretical debates developed (particularly over the relationship between consumption and production) need to be extended to the broader rural community. They must, moreover, be supported by empirical material providing detailed information on individual experiences within the household and the precise nature of social divisions.

The purpose of this paper is to begin to explore the nature of gender divisions within the rural community as one particular dimension of social 'cleavage' at the household level. In appreciation of the lack of evidence on the particular characteristics of gender divisions, the first tasks will be to provide a body of information on key areas of 'difference'. Such evidence will be interpreted in the light of theoretical debate about rural restructuring but will demonstrate how existing theory has partially obscured some important aspects of gender inequality and difference. This is particularly true of the restructuring of the rural labour process and while, as noted above, contemporary theoretical analyses have argued the need to acknowledge and explore gender relations in the context of rural change, the assumptions that have been made about the nature and course of rural restructuring have tended to preclude any real appreciation of gender difference or of the 'unevenness' of men and women's particular experiences.

The local labour market in rural areas has provided an important focus for the discussion of processes and outcomes associated with rural restructuring. It is a concept which allows, as Hadjimichalis and Vaiou (1990: 1) acknowledge the integration of 'global tendencies with the peculiarities of place'. It can be especially valuable in terms of the exploration of gender divisions, drawing in issues concerning the division of labour in the household and the negotiation of household strategies for economic and social reproduction. The following section will look briefly at some of the key areas of debate that have contributed to our understanding of the restructuring of the rural labour market. It will go on to demonstrate how such debates have underplayed the importance of gender relations within the household (in particular strategies for participating in formal employment) to the process of change in the rural labour market.

Rural restructuring and the labour market: current debate and new agendas

Changes in the agricultural economy, or more specifically, the location of investment and capital accumulation within agriculture have dominated studies of the restructuring of the rural labour market (see Marsden *et al.,* 1990; Kenny *et al.,* 1989; Lawrence, 1988). These changes have been discussed at a theoretical level in terms of a shift from Fordist to post-Fordist modes of production (see, for example, Cloke and Goodwin, 1992; Marsden and Murdoch, 1991) and have been seen as underpinning major changes in the relationship between production and consumption in rural areas and, as a result, the composition of the rural population. Empirical work in the UK, United States and Australia has helped to identify the scale and nature of changes in capital investment in rural areas and their implications for the rural labour market. Most recently authors have referred to a 'crisis' within agriculture as changes in investment by European and American governments have reinforced technology-driven shifts in patterns of capital accumulation.

Another well-documented area in terms of the restructuring of the rural labour market has been the creation of alternative employment opportunities in manufacturing and service sectors. Included here has been a very localised and patchy movement of manufacturing industry from urban areas to 'green field' sites within and beyond the urban fringe. Generally as a response to land and labour costs and availability, such relocation has again been theorised in terms of the application of a Fordist mode of production to rural areas. The more recent and also uneven increase in service sector employment (Thrist, 1987) has been seen by some to represent a movement to post-Fordism with all that this implies for employment practices and job 'flexibility'. The use of telecommunications has been seen as one particular facet of the restructuring of employment opportunities in rural areas (see Grimes, 1992) and of the relative importance of the service sector. Portrayed variably as the provider of valuable new jobs for those living in rural areas, or the 'high-tech' equivalent of the exploitative process of homeworking, teleworking is acknowledged as indicative of the incorporation of the rural economy into the wider circuits of capital accumulation and the national/international patterns of restructuring.

A third important focus here is the growing importance of self-employment and of the small family business/enterprise. In a detailed study of five different rural labour markets Errington *et al.* (1989) identified rates of self-employment that were significantly higher than the national rate at the time. In many ways self-employment is seen by both policy-makers and residents as highly appropriate for the rural labour market; it generally implies small-scale businesses, often 'craft' based or involving 'clean' new technologies. Self-employment is consequently seen as environmentally sound and less likely to pose a threat to rural conservation. Just as important are the associations between self-employment and the social relations of production. The image of the self-employed working for themselves and for the community, using family (and possibly village) labour is one which fits very well with the dominant ideology and value systems of rural communities (Whatmore *et al.*, 1991). It is the use of *family* labour that is obviously of particular interest here. As will be seen later, self-employment poses particular demands on the household not only in terms of the involvement of women in 'paid' work (and the renumeration of that work), but also in broader household decision-making strategies. Again, existing academic debate on social and economic relations within the rural family business has tended to be confined to the farm household.

While influential for the creation of employment opportunities in certain rural communities, the relocation of manufacturing and service industries into some rural areas should not be overemphasised. It has been widely recognised that far greater changes to the composition of the rural labour market have resulted, not from the creation of particular employment opportunities within rural areas *per se,* but from the rise in commuting and from changes to urban labour markets and to the labour process itself. Such changes have opened up many parts of rural Britain as potential residential locations for certain groups. The scale of rural immigration and its uneven development in terms of location and social class (and, to a lesser extent, age and ethnicity) have been well documented (see, for example, Bradley *et al.,* 1984; Cloke, 1992; Champion and Watkins, 1991; Cloke and Milbourne, 1992) as have its implications for traditional rural community structures. More recently research has started to explore the effects of middle-class 'colonisation' of rural spaces, not simply in terms of the practicalities of, for example, access to housing, but in relation to the appropriation of rural cultures and rural lifestyles that have been part of a commodification of rural living (Cloke and Goodwin, 1992).

There is insufficient time here for a detailed examination of these debates. However, there are a number of points that need to be highlighted since they are very relevant to the discussion of gender relations in the rural community that is developed below. The movement of middle-class 'fractions' into rural areas has been intricately tied in to a whole set of images and assumptions about rural spaces and to the social construction of rural communities. People have been attracted to rural living by the existence of a rural idyll (or perhaps several idylls) that their own presence in the community has then served to sustain. Detailed work on the nature of contemporary rural ideology has only recently begun to emerge (see Mingay, 1989; Mormont, 1990; Cloke and Milbourne, 1992). Such work has, however, demonstrated the strong links between the existence of a rural idyll and the 'use of the countryside as a new theatre of consumption' (Cloke and Goodwin, 1992: 328). In making these links work has been careful to stress the localised nature of both the character and the impact of the rural idyll.

The impact of the middle-class colonisation of rural space on the labour market clearly goes beyond simple issues of direct involvement. The position commanded by certain sections of the middle class within the national (and international) labour market has allowed them to play a key role in the recomposition of the rural economy and society and in particular the reorientation of rural communities from production to consumption. So while their access to rural areas has not in itself been determined primarily by their involvement in the local labour market, the middle class have succeeded in influencing that labour market through their control over power and decision-making and their ability to enforce their own choices in terms of lifestyles, culture, family values and so on.

Important steps have been taken towards advancing our understanding of the restructuring of the rural labour market – the forces of change and the implications for different groups in the rural population. As noted earlier in the paper, key questions concerning the differing experiences of individuals between and within households have yet to be explored. We know, as yet, very little about the gender inequalities resulting from the restructuring of the rural labour market; the impact of economic change on the relative levels of job opportunities between women and men, whether women and men have differing experiences of the growing 'flexibility' of the rural labour market. In addition we have yet to recognise the importance of gender relations on the nature of rural restructuring itself. By assuming (both implicity and explicity) that rural restructuring is driven largely by the economy, much existing work has implied some sort of direct causal relationship between economic and social change. In other words, where certain 'economic' processes are enacted, particular 'social' results will follow. The patterns of change that have become associated with rural restructuring will undoubtedly have implications for the realities and practicalities of women's involvement in paid work and also the broader operation of gender relations. But at the same time these patterns themselves are intricately tied up with, and shaped by, the changing gender relations within the rural community.

Just as important in the light of comments made above are questions concerning the role of gender relations in the development of rural spaces as sites of consumption. In order to understand more about the gendered nature of rural restructuring (in terms of its impact and *particular* characteristics) we need to know a lot more about household strategies for the creation of rural lifestyles amongst the middle and working classes. Critically, what role do gender relations within the household play in the ability (or desire) of that household to sustain a rural lifestyle? Given comments made elsewhere about the state's reinforcement of middle-class recomposition of rural spaces (see Cloke and Goodwin, 1992), a related question must be the extent to which household strategies for rural lifestyles have become institutionalised and encapsulated in policy. These are all substantial and complex issues which require investigation in their own right. In this paper it is the intention to concentrate on the impact of household strategies and the operation of gender relations on women's access to, and experience of, paid employment.

Debate around the family and the household has evolved primarily in the context of feminist theory. Such theory has argued, as Pratt and Hanson (1991: 55) acknowledge, that 'neither women's or men's work within the household or the labour force can be conceptualised adequately without a clear understanding of household arrangements and strategies'. There are now a considerable number of studies in the literature which demonstrate the constraints on women's involvement in the labour market as a result of demands from the household and the division of labour within it (see, for example, Hamilton and Barrett, 1986; Mackenzie and Rose, 1983). Such work has been developed at a theoretical level in discussions around the relationship between production and consumption and the domestic labour debate. Recently, research has looked more specifically at household relations in the context of economic restructuring (Rubery and Tarling, 1988; Pahl and Wallace, 1985; McDowell, 1992). Here work has investigated the household survival strategies that have been utilised – particularly work in the informal economy – in response to the decline in traditional forms of employment. Such strategies have frequently involved an increase in women's involvement in paid work and a greater dependence on informal networks of support for domestic work and child care.

Some of the issues raised by feminist analysis in relation to household strategies in restructuring economies are applied here to the study of rural areas. The aim is to provide some much needed empirical detail on the involvement of women in the rural labour process, identifying what sort of jobs they are involved in and the conditions under which they work. Other studies of women's participation in paid work in the context of economic restructuring have drawn attention, as noted above, to the 'flexibilisation' of employment and to the importance of women taking up new opportunities, especially in terms of 'crisis' in the economic survival of the household. Issues around flexibilisation are clearly important in the analysis of the rural labour process. The purpose of examining women's involvement in paid work is to identify whether changes in work practices and employment availability (in line with those associated with increased flexibility elsewhere) have had an impact on the actual experiences of women in the labour market.

The main contribution of this chapter, however, lies in its efforts to link the detail of women's employment experience to gender relations in the household. Issues around both the practical undertaking of domestic tasks and the influence of values to the division of labour in the household are discussed. It is argued that decisions about the involvement of both men and women in the labour market are heavily influenced by strategies devised by the household in pursuit of certain goals and values. Beliefs about rural lifestyles and cultures from an important input to these household goals and thus to the negotiation of employment participation. The analysis demonstrates the way in which locational decisions made by the households generally reflect the prioritisation of male employment and lifestyle choices. Decisions by immigrants to move to a rural locality tend to be made at certain stages of the life-cycle when the sorts of values reflected in the dominant rural ideology – especially those surrounding the family and the division of labour in the household – have particular meaning. Attempts are made here to go some way towards identifying the implications of such decisions for women's current involvement in waged work and their future work possibilities.

Women and the rural labour market

Data informing this analysis of women's participation in the rural labour market are drawn from a questionnaire survey undertaken in three different rural areas of England.[1] It was felt to be important to undertake the research in different 'types' of rural area in order to reflect the very different ways in which individual localities have experienced the process of restructuring. The areas chosen represent, between them, very different patterns of capital exploitation and social change and consequently very different pressures on local labour markets. Job opportunities in each of the areas reflect these differing histories. Variations in local cultures, politics and community development have also been important in shaping local social and economic relations and although this research was unable to explore such variations in any great detail, it does recognise their influence over the wider processes of economic change.

The study areas (see Figure 1.1) included firstly, the Kennet district of Wiltshire – a highly accessible area representing many of the characteristics associated with rural areas in the 'commuter belt' of southern England; little male unemployment, a high proportion of professional households, high property prices and competition for housing and a relatively large number of recent immigrants, many of whom are employed in the service sector. Secondly, North Cornwall – a more socially and economically diverse area where high levels of immigration have been tempered recently by poor job opportunities (male unemployment in the study parishes was slightly higher than the national rate). Thirdly, Bolsover district of Derbyshire – an area dominated by (ex) mining villages and high male unemployment. The population of this study as a whole had experienced far lower levels of immigration than either Kennet or North Cornwall.

Women in paid employment

Women's participation in paid work over the three study areas fell well short of the national rate with a total of 54 per cent of women interviewed having a paid job compared with 71 per cent nationally in 1991 (Department of Employment, 1992). There was significant variation between study areas; Cornwall was closest to the national figure with 61 per cent of women interviewed in employment, then Wiltshire with 52 per cent and Derbyshire with just 47 per cent. While these figures serve to support the claim that women's activity rates are generally lower in rural areas than in towns and cities, they tell us little in isolation and must be analysed in the light of other data on the characteristics of women's involvement in the rural labour market.

In contrast to the basic activity levels, the number of women employed part-time in the study areas was found to be higher than the national rate. In 1991 41.8 per cent of women in Britain worked on a part-time basis (defined as 17 hours a week or less), while in the three study areas the figure ranged from 70 per cent in Derbyshire to 51 per cent in Cornwall. The particularly high instance of part-time work amongst rural women is important and says much

Figure 1.1 Location of study parishes

Table 1.1 Occupational categories of women in employment in the study parishes

Occupational group	Social class	% of women		
		Wilts	**Cornwall**	**Derbys**
Professional	1	1	0	0
Intermediate non-manual	2	36	37	19
Skilled manual	3	39	33	35
Semi-skilled, factory and domestic	4	14	23	35
Unskilled	5	8	6	10

(*Source:* Questionnaire survey, 1990)

about the choices available to women together with the constraints and pressures that they are under. There is considerable evidence in the literature linking part-time work with poor employment conditions (see Beechey and Perkins, 1987; Walby, 1988). Given the high incidence of part-time work here, one of the most pressing questions was whether the same relationship between *quality* of work and hours was repeated. A related issue concerns the status of women who were employed in the family business. A surprisingly high number of women claimed to be working for their husband's or the family business – almost 20 per cent of those interviewed in Cornwall, for example. The terms of women's involvement in such businesses varied enormously with consequent implications for hours and pay. Some were employed for a wage in a formal capacity while others seemed to work when needed and were either unpaid or received wages as and when the business could afford it.

The *type* of work women in the three study areas were involved in was analysed and classified according to occupational groupings and social class. Overall women who were in employment tended to be disproportionately concentrated in jobs in clerical and sales work, teaching, medical and social work. Less than 1 per cent of the women questioned worked in professional/managerial jobs (those classified as social class 1). A comparison between those employed full-time and those working part-time revealed a particular concentration of part-time jobs within the lower social economic groups. Breaking down employment structure by study area showed that while there was a fair degree of consistency between the proportion of the workforce in social class 3, other categories demonstrated more variation. In Wiltshire greater numbers of women worked in the higher occupational groups (professional and non-manual), while there were fewer in employed in semi-skilled and unskilled work (see Table 1.1). By contrast, the employment structures in Cornwall and Derbyshire were more heavily weighted in favour of these lower class groups. This was particularly noticable in Derbyshire where 35 per cent of women worked in semi-skilled/factory/domestic work and a further 10 per cent in unskilled work (see Table 1.1).

What is interesting in the context of these figures is the numbers of women responding to the questionnaire who had formal qualifications (either educational or job-related skills) which they were not using in their current job. Over half the women interviewed said that they had formal qualifications – these women were largely concentrated in Wiltshire and, to a lesser degree, in Cornwall – but of these, less than 50 per cent used their qualifications in their current work. Many instances were found in which highly qualified women (with degrees or a high level of specialist training) were doing work – often clerical or secretarial – that could have been done by a far less well qualified person. While there was little difference between part-time and full-time workers in terms of the proportion of women who actually possessed qualifications, full-timers were much more likely to be using their qualifications in their present job.

It might be argued by some that accepting low-skill (and often low-status) jobs is a 'choice' that many women make at certain stages of the life-cycle and, given the apparent acceptance of the situation (few respondents, when asked, said that they would prefer a more challenging job) not an issue. What was evident from the questionnaire, however, was that women's acceptance derived from a deep-seated belief that, if they wanted to have children, a career and even employment *per se* had to be sacrificed. They saw themselves as 'lucky to have something', an attitude that extended to the *conditions* under which women worked as well as to what jobs they did.[2] Women's concentration in low-status employment was reinforced by very chequered work histories. Only a small percentage of women were engaged on what could be called a career path – in other words progressing through jobs to better paid, higher status employment. Most women described fragmented employment backgrounds and only one-third had been in their current jobs for two years or more. In Wiltshire it appeared that, of those women returning to paid work after the birth of their children, 58 per cent went back to a different type of job to that that they had previously, while less than 10 per cent actually returned to work for the same employer.

Conditions of women's employment in rural areas

Having established the extent and form of women's direct participation in the labour market, the research went on to look more closely at the conditions under which women worked. The first issue, pay, is notoriously difficult to evaluate due partly to the reluctance of individuals to divulge information but also because of the different ways in which women were paid (the problem, for example, of those working casually for the family business). Another difficulty was the irregularity of women's employment in terms of hours and the significant daily and weekly variations that this imposed). The analysis of wage rates, while a little speculative, did bring out some clear trends that are worth recording here. Levels of pay across the study areas can be described as generally, but not universally, low. There were instances (in Wiltshire and Cornwall) of some relatively high salaries being earned, although only four women in all were found to be working for more than £15,000 a year. There was far more evidence of women working for very low wages. In neither Derbyshire nor Cornwall were there any women whose weekly wage exceeded the Equal Opportunities Commission's 'average' wage of £168 for a 37-hour week. In Cornwall four women were found to be working a 40-hour week for less than £100. Many of the respondents in Cornwall commented on the relatively low wages that were paid in the region (some cited examples of jobs that were paid at a far lower level in Cornwall than 'up country'). The feeling seemed to be that £2.50 an hour was a good wage and that those women working in jobs where there was a nationally fixed rate (home helps, for example, received £3.40 per hour) were seen as exceptional and 'very lucky'. Competition for such jobs was enormous and the source of considerable resentment amongst the women who had lived in the locality all their lives.

As well as recording the general incidence of low wages, the survey also revealed poor job security, low levels of paid holiday and time off for illness. While few women questioned believed their jobs to be under immediate threat, less than half had a written contract of employment (ranging from 32 per cent of employed women in Cornwall to 58 per cent in Wiltshire). An important discrepancy was found to exist in all areas between full-time and part-time employees. In Cornwall, for example, 43 per cent of women working full-time had a contract of employment as opposed to 23 per cent of those working on a part-time basis and in general across the whole survey population those employed in full-time positions were twice as likely to have a contract of employment. A similar pattern emerged with respect to paid holiday and sick pay. In general the conditions overall were poorer in the rural areas; only 52 per cent of respondents received paid holiday entitlements while 46 per cent received pay for time they were away from work due to illness (the national rates in 1984 were estimated to be 88 per cent and 67 per cent respectively) (Martin and Roberts, 1984). Again a significant difference was found to exist between full- and part-time workers with the latter being much less likely to be entitled to holiday and sickness pay.

The picture emerging from the analysis of labour-market characteristics is of a limited range of employment opportunities available to women in the rural study areas – particularly jobs requiring higher levels of skill/qualifications and offering good pay and working conditions. Women's inability to command employment at this level is, it seems, due partly to the absence of job opportunities in the areas (almost half of the women not currently in employment stated that they would like to have a job at the current time although only a small number of these were actually registered as unemployed or actively seeking paid work), but also to another set of constraints not determined by the rural labour market alone. To elaborate on the first of these issues, job availability, it is important to return to the rural restructuring debate discussed earlier in the paper, especially in the context of differences occurring between study areas.

As has been noted, the restructuring process impacts differently in different locations and, indeed, the three rural case study locations selected for this research were intended to reflect some of these differences. Without detailing the exact characteristics of social and economic change within the study areas, it is clear in looking simply at the data on male employment and unemployment that recent capital investment in the vicinity of the study parishes has varied considerably. Women's employment did reflect, to some extent, differences in the broader labour-market characteristics of the study areas. In Wiltshire there were more women employed on higher wages, in professional jobs, for example. In Cornwall there was a greater emphasis on casual employment – often in the tourist trade or other parts of the service sector. Such work was generally less 'secure' and more poorly paid than equivalent grade jobs in Wiltshire. In Derbyshire women were concentrated in the manual, semi-skilled sectors and while their jobs were not perhaps 'secure' (in the true sense of the word), they were nevertheless generally *regular* jobs with set hours and conditions.

Having noted the differences between women in the three study parishes, however, what was also striking was the extent of the similarities in women's position within the labour market. Given the differences in general labour-market trends between the study areas, it had been anticipated that rather more variation would be found in women's participation in the different localities. Variation between areas in terms of what women actually did appeared to be overshadowed by the similarities which existed in their experience of paid work – the level of wages, conditions of employment and their over qualification for the jobs being done. The patterns emerging in the experience of rural women in terms of access to, and conditions within, employment demonstrate very strongly the need to look beyond changes occurring within the labour market by way of explanation. In the second part of the research women were questioned about other constraints on their involvement in the labour market and about aspects of their domestic lives in an attempt to discover something of the impact of gender relations on women's employment in rural areas.

Analysing women's employment in this way is not intended to argue the existence of two separate and mutually exclusive sets of social and economic processes – one driven by economic restructuring and one by gender relations. It is, however, to reinforce the point that the whole direction and character of change that has occurred as a result of the relocation of capital investment incorporates an important gender dimension. The impact of restructuring is not only reflected in gender divisions but is also determined by them. Complex issues surrounding consumption patterns – their articulation, for example, with class divisions and social status – incorporate very strong beliefs as to the division of labour and power between genders. Women's involvement in the labour market cannot be divorced from these beliefs and power relations. The conditions under which women are able to enter employment are bound up in a package of gender relations and embodied in household strategies which are themselves intrinsically incorporated in the process of rural restructuring.

Gender relations and women's employment

Returning more directly to the influence of gender relations on women's paid work it is important to note, firstly, the high incidence of conventional household structures within the survey population. Over 90 per cent of respondents came from nuclear families in which the male partner (in virtually every case stated as 'husband') was the chief bread winner. By the same token, fewer than 5 per cent of women lived alone, with friends or with just their children. The importance of the male partner's employment was clearly demonstrated by the high number of respondents, especially in Wiltshire and Cornwall, who cited 'husband's job'as the main reason for the family moving to the area. An interesting dimension to this issue is the number of families who moved to the village to facilitate the husband starting his own (or the family) business. In no single case of relocation was the woman's own job the cause of the family's move, emphasising the point that the employment of rural women only rarely appeared as part of a career path but was a much more random reflection of job availability and life-cycle position in a particular place and time. Consequently, few women questioned had returned to the same job (or even the same career) after stopping work to have children. Where the family had moved to the area with the intention of embarking on a 'family business' women's labour (where used directly) was mainly confined to secretarial and book-keeping work. While no special study was made of this area in the research (undoubtedly an important issue for further work), it seemed that women were unlikely to play an *equal* role in decision-making within the business.

'Starting a family' was the most common reason given by women not currently in employment for leaving work, while the continuation of childcare responsibilities the most important influence over their ability/willingness to return to the labour market. The close relationship between childcare and employment participation and the added constraint imposed by the lack of childcare provision in rural areas has been discussed elsewhere (see Little, 1986; 1987). This research allowed something of the *scale* of the problem to be appreciated. Twenty per cent of employed women in Cornwall, 25 per cent of those in Wiltshire and 50 per cent in Derbyshire reported that they experienced regular problems with the childcare arrangements that they made in order to have a paid job.

Comparatively few women interviewed in the course of the research made use of formal, paid childcare provision. In Wiltshire 22 per cent of employed women with young children used a childminder and just 5 per cent took their children to a nursery. Much greater use was made of informal help from family and friends (40 per cent) while a significant proportion of employed women (33 per cent) said that they worked from home to enable them to look after their children (or they worked from friend's houses where they could have their children with them). This pattern was also repeated in the other two study areas; in Cornwall just 7 per cent of employed women with young children used paid childcare provision, 23 per cent worked from home or took their children with them to work (without proper childcare facilities).

There were three main reasons for such a low dependence on formal paid childcare. Firstly, the lack of appropriate childcare provision available in the village or in the locality. On this issue women were quick to point out that to be of use to most of them childcare needed to be very *accessible* and that meant the same parish as home or work. A second reason for the low takeup of paid childcare was that women simply couldn't afford it. The expectation in the vast majority of cases was that it was the women and not the family/household who took responsibility for paying for childcare. Consequently, the low wages earned by women in rural areas frequently made paying for childcare impossible. Several women (predominently in Cornwall where wage rates were particularly low) said that the cost of paying for childcare meant that it was not worth their while taking a paid job since a substantial proportion (and for some all) of their wages would be spent on childcare. The third and less common (though still significant) reason for the low uptake of paid childcare was the belief that mothers themselves should be personally responsible for the care of their children and that to pay for help at a nursery or childminder was somehow failing in their duties as a mother. This attitude seemed to exist amongst both middle-class and working-class women and while obviously not unique to rural women can be linked to more conventional patterns of household structure and attitudes towards 'the family' that are discernable in rural areas (see Little, 1987). There is also the issue of community size – the smallness of rural populations encouraging women to feel that their childcare practices were under scrutiny by other women in the community and that in being seen to send their children to a childminder they may be thought to be 'poor mothers'.

In other areas of domestic work the questionnaire again revealed some very traditional attitudes towards the gender division of labour. More than half the women interviewed in each study area said that they did *all* the housework and shopping with no help from anyone else in the household; in Derbyshire the proportion was as high as 78 per cent. The hiring of help from outside the home for domestic work was not surprisingly linked to social class; in Wiltshire 17 per cent of respondents said that they had paid help in the home while in Derbyshire the figure was only 5 per cent. Interestingly, women's participation in paid employment did not appear to influence whether or not paid help in the home was recruited indicating its possible role as a status symbol.

Those women who did not have a paid job at the time of the research were asked about the reasons for this and about their future plans. The vast majority gave 'taking care of the family' as the reasons for their current lack of employment, although a small percentage, as noted above, said that they were actively seeking work and/or were registered as unemployed. Much greater numbers of women (over 50 per cent of those not in waged work in Cornwall and Derbyshire and one-third of those in Wiltshire) said that they would like to have a paid job in the future. There appeared, from talking to women, to be little questioning of the possible alternatives to their current roles. While a minority did cite the lack of suitable employment opportunities or the absence of accessible and affordable childcare as the reasons for their lack of employment, it seemed generally that giving up a career was a decision made by women when they started a family. This can also, at least amongst immigrants, be linked to a wider package of life-cycle decisions made by households that included moving to the countryside. There were again clearly class differences here with this pattern of leaving the labour market much more common amongst middle-class residents for whom the opportunity to exercise choice was less financially constrained. Some women spoke of the pressures on them to remain at home with their children – examples were cited where husbands of both middle- and working-class women had been opposed to their wives returning to work. In Derbyshire several women were interviewed while on a word-processing course that was designed to improve their work-related skills and make them more 'employable'. Most of the eight women on this course had not told their husbands that they were attending for fear that they would not be 'allowed' to come.

The following employment and family history of two respondents demonstrate a number of typical issues and attitudes which surround the participation of women in paid work. The issues identified are not unique to these women but appeared with consistency amongst the questionnaire respondents. They demonstrate that while household decisions are clearly influenced by class position they also incorporate strong pressures resulting from the operation of gender relations.

'Sue', lived with her husband and two children in Wiltshire. They had moved to the village from just outside London when Sue's husband obtained promotion in the accountancy firm for which he worked. Before the family moved Sue worked in a well-paid job as a PR consultant for which she had acquired various formal qualifications and had several years training. On moving to Wiltshire Sue gave up her job to 'start a family'. She did not think of going back to work after having the children mainly because she wanted to stay at home and care for them but also because she was 'required' to attend (and host) social functions connected with her husband's business. Now that the children are older (in their teens) Sue has started to work part-time. She is employed in a small local company as a secretary/typist where she earns a 'fairly poor' wage. She is frustrated that she has skills that she isn't using yet feels that she has lost the confidence to return to the sort of high-powered work that she did previously. She has no doubts about the priorities that she adopted in the past yet feels that her talents and experience are now wasted. Had she lived in an urban area she believes that the range of local opportunities would have allowed her to get back into the sort of work she was doing previously. As it is she considers herself fortunate to have a regular job, close to home working for a reasonably flexible employer.

'Carol' is a working-class married woman living in a local authority house in the Derbyshire study area. Carol's husband was made redundant when the local coal mine closed and has been unemployed for several months with no immediate prospect of employment. At the time of the research, Carol was enroled on a word-processing course at a local college. She attended the course without her husband's knowledge as he 'disapproved' of the idea of her getting a paid job. Carol currently *did* work as a cleaner but only for a couple of hours a week. She felt that although, once she'd completed her course, there would be opportunities for full-time work, her husband's attitude and the need for her to be at home when her children came home from school would probably prevent her from getting a job. 'Restructuring' of the local economy has seen a shift from primary to tertiary employment, providing opportunities for women like Carol. For some, however, household strategies, reflecting very traditional values and gender role assumptions, have prevented them taking up such opportunities.

These cases raise a whole range of questions concerning the constraints on women's participation in waged work and demonstrate the complexity of the relationship between different factors. These case histories and others not included here serve to emphasise in particular the need to look closely at the relationship between labour market changes and the availability of employment opportunities and gender relations which impinge on the uptake of opportunities. Some of these issues are taken up below.

Conclusions

This brief analysis of women's employment in the rural labour market has sought to clarify some of the major characteristics of their participation and in doing so to contribute to the wider understanding of rural restructuring. The conclusions that have been reached are very tentative reflecting both the small-scale nature of the research and the previous neglect of gender issues in the study of social and economic restructuring in rural areas. Having said this some important patterns have emerged from the work that provide at least a starting point for future theoretical and empirical work in this area.

It is clear from the evidence discussed here that women's participation in employment in rural areas is bound up, not only in the availability of, and access to, jobs in such areas, but also in the operation of gender relations within the household and community. This is hardly a new assertion – it was noted earlier that feminist analyses of economic restructuring have been quick to point out the role of the household in determining women's position in the labour market. What is interesting here is the way in which gender relations in the household and the strategies adopted to accommodate paid and unpaid work are strongly influenced by both the image and reality of rural lifestyles. Popular perceptions about rural living appear to create a greater acceptance or tolerance of the lack of employment opportunities for women while the importance of the family, the community and the role of women as mothers ensure that their careers generally assume second place.

The values held by both middle-class and working-class households prioritised the male partner (husband) as principal, and often sole, bread winner as the wider survey and the case histories demonstrated. Frequently women's own careers were sacrificed to enable them to support their husbands. This support took the form of caring for children, entertaining business clients, working in the 'family' business and acting as an unpaid secretary. Interestingly, the notion of self employment seemed to fit, especially amongst the middle class, very comfortably with the acceptable rural lifestyle. Again, self employment for men frequently meant support being provided by women members of the household. The picture which emerged from the research appears to challenge the quite widely held notion of a rural 'service class'. Little evidence was found here to support the idea that rural households are overwhelmingly represented by double-income couples in which both partners hold well-paid professional and permanent jobs. There were some examples of professional couples in the surveys undertaken but these were firmly in the minority. Far more common were cases where women had given up professional jobs in their mid 20s only to return to lower grade, or non-professional, employment or to remain outside the labour market altogether.

Women's role within the traditional rural ideology – as perceived by many households (especially, but not exclusively, middle-class households) extended beyond the immediate family into the community. Women's labour and 'caring skills' were provided, on an unpaid basis, in the communities studied in a number of ways. As well as caring for their own children, women frequently assisted other women, both on an individual basis but also as supplementary help in local primary schools. Women also cared for elderly people within the parishes – again through both formal and informal networks – and assisted in the running of other village groups, many of which had a caring function. Women's activities of this kind within the community are clearly a very important part of the dominant rural ideology. As such they have become, in some instances, institutionalised by state policy (or more accurately the lack of it). Informal care has replaced formal facilities in many areas (child care and care of the aged being the most obvious). In rural areas, the expectations surrounding women's willingness to participate in such activities are particularly high. Women's involvement in these 'village-based' activities helps to assimilate new households into the community and consequently are frequently supported by the household – taking priority in some cases over women's participation in paid work. Women themselves acquire personal satisfaction from their involvement in community networks since it confirms their expectations about village life and reinforces their belief in their own household strategies, goals and values.

There is little doubt that the study of rural labour markets has been enhanced by the more global perspective that has been adopted in the debates around rural restructuring. The application of these perspectives to the local economy and society of rural areas has helped in the recognition of divisions and cleavages within the rural community but at the same time provided a level of explanation that goes beyond the specificity of the individual locality. Work in this area has encouraged the use and development of social theory and in particular class analysis (see Cloke and Thrift, 1990) as a way of interpreting and understanding the complex social and economic relations that characterise rural areas. It has also drawn attention to the importance of state-society relationships and to local political divisions to the distribution of power and wealth within the changing rural community.

The issues raised here have highlighted the importance of a specific focus on gender relations in terms of our understanding of the process and impact of rural restructuring. In examining gender relations attention must be directed towards the household and the strategies used to negotiate the differing demands of paid and unpaid work. More research is needed on the actual choices made by different households (and by different members of the household) in the pursuit of rural lifestyles, and on the interaction between these choices and the rural spaces. Questions concerning the nature of consumption – its reflection, for example, in the built environment and attitudes towards development – and its impact on the process of restructuring are critical to the involvement of individuals in the labour market and the negotiation of household strategies.

Notes

1. The information used here was collected as part of a research project funded by the Rural Development Commission. The arguments put forward here, however, are the author's own.
2. It should be noted, as a proviso to this discussion, that this analysis has adopted a traditional and, it could be argued, male attitude to what constitutes 'skill' in this context. Many women questioned while not in possession of formal educational or professional qualifications, did demonstrate (and require) a range of skills – in particular caring- related skills – in the course of their work. Unfortunately, despite their importance, these skills are rarely recognised in any formal sense that is reflected in either pay or status.

References

Beechey, V. and Perkins, T. (1987) *A Matter of Hours: Women, part-time work and the labour market.* Polity Press, London.

Bradley, T., Lowe, P. and Wright, S. (1984) *Deprivation and Welfare in Rural Areas.* Geo Books, Norwich.

Champion, A. and Watkins, C. (eds) (1991) *People in the Countryside.* Paul Chapman Publishers, London.

Cloke, P. (1992) The countryside: development, conservation an increasingly marketable commodity. In Cloke (ed.) *Policy and Change in Thatcher's Britain.* Pergamon Press, Oxford.

Cloke, P. and Goodwin, M. (1992) Conceptualising countryside change: from post-Fordism to rural structured coherence. *Transaction of the Institute of British Geographers,* 17: 321–36.

Cloke, P. and Milbourne, P. (1992) Deprivation and lifestyles in rural Wales. Rurality and the cultural dimension. *Journal of Rural Studies,* 8(4): 359–71.

Cloke, P. and Milbourne, P. (1993) IBG paper.

Cloke, P. and Thrift, N. (1990) Class and change in rural Britain. In Marsden, T., Lowe, P. and Whatmore, S. (eds) *Rural Restructuring: Global Processes and their Responses.* David Fulton Publishers, London.

Delphy, C. (1984) *Close to Home.* Hutchinson, London.

Department of Employment (1992) *Labour Market Statistics, 1991.* HMSO, London.

Errington, A., Bennett, R. and Marshall, B. (1989) *Employment and Training in Rural Areas.* Rural Development Commission, London.

Grimes, S. (1992) Exploiting information and communication technologies for rural development. *Journal of Rural Studies,* 8(3): 269–78.

Hadjimichalis, C. and Vaiou, D. (1990) Flexible labour markets and regional development in northern Greece. *International Journal of Urban and Regional Research,* 14: 1–23.

Hamilton, R. and Barrett, M. (1986) *The Politics of Diversity.* Verso, London.

Kenney, M., Lobao, I., Curry, J. and Goe, R. (1989) Midwestern agriculture in US Fordism: from New Deal to economic restructuring. *Sociologis Ruralis,* 29: 139–48.

Lawrence, L. (1988) *Capitalism and the Countryside.* Pluto, Sydney.

Little, J. (1986) Feminist perspectives in rural geography: an introduction. *Journal of Rural Studies,* 2: 1–8.

Little, J. (1987) Gender relations in rural areas: the importance of women's domestic role. *Journal of Rural Studies,* 3: 335–42.

Lowe, P., Marsden, T. and Munton, R. (1990) The social and economic restructuring of rural Britain: a position statement. Working Paper 2 ESRC Countryside Change Working Paper Series, Department of Agricultural Economics, University of Newcastle.

McDowell, L. (1992) Social divisions, income inequality and gender relations in the 1980s. In Cloke, P. (ed.) *Policy and Change in Thatcher's Britain.* Pergamon Press, Oxford.

Mackenzie, S. and Rose, D. (1983) Industrial change, the domestic economy and home life. In Anderson, J., Duncan, S. and Hudson, R. (eds) *Redundant Spaces in Cities and Regions.* Academic Press, New York.

McLaughlin, B. (1986) The rhetoric and reality of rural deprivation. *Journal of Rural Studies,* 2: 291–308.

Marsden, T., Lowe, P. and Whatmore, S. (1990) Introduction: questions of rurality. In Marsden, T. *et al.,* (eds.) *Rural Restructuring: Global Processes and their Responses.* David Fulton Publishers, London.

Martin, J. and Roberts, C. (1984) *Women and Employment: A Lifetime Perspective.* Department of Employment, HMSO.

Mingay (1989) *The Rural Idyll.* Routledge, London.

Mormont, M. (1990) Who is rural? Or how to be rural: towards a sociology of the rural. In Marsden, T. *et al.,* (eds.) *Rural Restructuring: Global Processes and their Responses.*

Murdoch, J. and Marsden, T. (1991) Reconstituting the Rural in an Urban Region: Social and Economic Change in the Buckinghamshire Countryside. Paper presented at the Urban Change and Conflict Conference, Lancaster, 1991.

Pahl, R. and Wallace, C. (1985) Household work strategies in economic recession. In Redclift, N. and Migione, E. (eds) *Beyond Employment: Household, Gender and Subsistence.* Blackwell, Oxford.

Pratt, G. and Hanson, S. (1991) On the links between home and work: family household strategies in a buoyant labour market. *International Journal of Urban and Regional Research,* 15: 55–74.

Redclift, N. and Whatmore, S. (1990) Household, consumption and livelihood: ideologies and issues in rural research. In Marsden *et al.,* (eds) *Rural Restructuring: Global Processes and their Responses.* David Fulton Publishers, London.

Rubery, J. and Tarling, R. (1988) Women's employment in declining Britain. In Rubery, J. (ed.) *Women and Recession.* Routledge, London.

Thrift, N. (1987) Manufacturing rural geography. *Journal of Rural Studies,* 3: 77–81.

Urry, J. (1984) Capitalist restructuring, recomposition and the regions. In Bradley, T. and Lowe, P. (eds) *Locality and Rurality.* Geo Books, Norwich.

Walby, S. (1988) *Gender Segregation at Work.* Polity Press, London.

Whatmore, S. (1991) *Farming Women: Gender, Work and Family Enterprise.* Macmillan, London.

Whatmore, S., Lowe, P. and Marsden, T. (1991) Artisan or entrepreneur? Re-fashioning rural production. Introduction to *Rural Enterprise, Shifting Perspectives on Small-scale Production:* 1–11. David Fulton Publishers, London.

CHAPTER 2

Contesting Rurality: Country Women's Social and Political Networks

Elizabeth Teather

Introduction

This chapter will examine the ways in which rural women's organisations contribute to the social production of space, and specifically their active involvement in shaping the meaning and representation of rurality. What do their members understand by 'rural'? How does the rural context influence their selection of goals? Conversely, are their activities altering the attributes of 'rurality' and the social structures associated with rural communities? What ideology characterises such organisations and how do their organisational structures reflect this ideology? What differences are there between types of rural women's organisations and the contribution they make to the transformation of gender relations in their local and wider communities?

Rural women's organisations institutionalise and deploy particular rural visions of life in pursuit of different social and political agendas. A distinction will be drawn between those that are concerned to defend the status quo and those committed to challenging the gender regime that typifies rural communities, with its particularly marked pattern of male hegemony. The newer, non-traditional rural women's organisations studied here represent women farmers who are committed to gaining recognition as farmers in their own right and to becoming part of the decision-making structures of the agricultural industry. Both these, and the far older, traditional rural women's organisations, affirm the economic and social unit of the family farm, and work devotedly in a variety of ways on and off the farm for its continued existence. The older organisations have a broader commitment to rural, not just farming, communities, and to their perception of the 'rural way of life' which includes, but is not limited to, farming. Compared with the newer organisations, they are far larger but are not able to recruit new, young members in significant numbers, and face a period of significant decline as members age. They are clearly not at the forefront of the transformative aspect of the rural restructuring process, but play an equally important part in affirming, often quite vocally, traditional gender relations and concepts of masculinity and femininity.

The role of social networks needs examining in the context of the severe economic restraints currently operating on commercial family farms in Australasia, North America and Europe. In New South Wales, Australia, for example, many families in recent years have sold up or walked off their properties, often suffering personal trauma. The service centre function of many small towns has been dramatically reduced (Lawrence, 1990; Taylor, 1991). In these circumstances, social networks of all kinds adopt a role that is, perhaps, even more significant than in times of prosperity (Fitchen, 1991). The various networks represent a crucially important aspect of social cohesion, knitting members of demoralised communities together by reinforcing and maintaining shared ideologies, lobbying on behalf of members and their communities, and offering opportunities for mutually supportive social interaction of like-minded people. But, equally, such circumstances mean that organisations seeking to transform aspects of society are not likely to receive a sympathetic response. Even, this inhospitable climate has not prevented newer women's networks from pressing their agenda of challenging male hegemony, particularly within the agricultural industry.

Rural women's organisations, spatiality and the structuration process

Rural women's networks represent threads of one colour woven into the dense, multicoloured fabric of rural society. For the moment, this metaphor suffices to capture the sense of a network as a matrix comprising lines of contact between individuals. While it is important to grasp the pattern of the weave – the way networks are organised – it is perhaps more important to be aware of the process of continuing transformation that the cloth – rural society – is undergoing. As we look on, the interconnections of threads, the dyes, the woven patterns, the quality and origin of warp and weft, the texture of the fabric, all shimmer as in a mirage that gradually develops from one image into a new one and into yet another, irreversibly – but not inevitably towards one end, because the weavers' creativity and deliberate act of decision-making combine to affect the direction of the transformation process.

This image captures the process of 'spatiality': the idea of space as socially produced, as opposed to 'the physical space of material nature and the mental space of cognition and representation' (Soja, 1985: 92–3). Soja's concept of spatiality encompasses social space (the woven cloth), time (the running of the loom) and human agency (the weaver). Social science, and human geography in particular, has always had problems handling the analysis of environments in a state of perpetual transformation through human agency at the same time as having a physical dynamic of their own (this physical dynamic is an aspect that the loom metaphor fails to capture). As Soja puts it:

> The production of space is . . . not simply a mechanical extrusion of a frozen matrix which acts passively to contain society. Spatiality and temporality, human geography and human history, intersect in a complex social process which creates a constantly evolving historical sequence of spatialities, a spatio-temporal structuration of social life which gives form not only to the grand movements of societal development but also to the recursive practices of day-to-day activity.
>
> The production of space (and the making of history) can thus be described as both the medium and the outcome of social action and relationship. (Soja, 1985: 94)

'Social action and relationship' comprise countless interactions, formal and informal, structured and unstructured, deliberate, spontaneous or unexpected. Structured organisations, like the networks to be examined, are examples of agents in the process of spatiality. When individuals in one or more communities organise to achieve certain objectives, the resulting group comprises a voluntary association. Such associations tend to be characterised by certain patterns of ideological commitment, in terms, for example, of political alignment or of attitudes towards feminism. Rural women's organisations are no exception. Examination of such ideologies is a necessary component of understanding the social production of space, because particular sets of values establish the framework for decision-making and for the lobbying process. 'The production of ideas (and ideologies) is thus an important component of the production of spatiality' (Soja, 1985: 94). Older schools of sociological theory are useful here. Organised groups, Bott claims (1971: 58), may develop a distinctive sub-culture. 'The members of organised groups are likely to develop a high degree of consensus on norms and identity because of their frequent interaction with one another' (Bott, 1971: 223). As traditional women's networks in Australia, Canada, Britain and New Zealand have been established for over seventy years, they have developed highly distinctive ideologies. Women who feel uncomfortable about this ideology do not join. Static or falling membership in such organisations indicates that they are not at the forefront of social change, actively transforming spatialities, but their role as tenacious agents resisting change is an important one in the contemporary social reconstruction of rurality.

Spatiality, then, is a theoretical construct that assists in the interpretation of the significance and operation of rural networks operating as influential agents in environments that have a social as well as a physical dynamic. But there is another, complementary approach that adds clarity and power to the concept of spatiality: the structuration theory postulated by Giddens. To the older and somewhat deterministic, structural view of society, Giddens adds the transformative element of knowledgeable human agency, and sees a 'duality of structure' in which '[n]either structure nor action can exist independently' (Haralambos, 1990: 815). The term 'structuration' is used by Giddens 'to describe the way that structures relate to social actions'; by 'duality of structure' he invokes the process by which 'structures make social action possible, [but] at the same time . . . social action creates those very structures' (Haralambos, 1990: 815). The intense commitment of the rural women's organisations studied in this chapter to either changing or maintaining the status quo can be seen in the light of the structuration process, and it will be shown that the reproduction of social structures, in modified form or more or less as before, lies at the heart of their missions.

Urry comments that organisations may become powerful lobbies involved in defending or challenging social structures: 'changes are achieved only through collective forms of struggle and not through individual efforts, in particular, through trade unions, political parties and pressure groups of various sorts' (Urry, 1981: 128). Urry also clarifies the relationship between structures and structuration. He suggests that 'there is always a diversity of bases upon which individuals may mobilise' and that 'the main dimensions of structuration in [a] generally descending order of importance' are:

1. Spatial organisation of labour and residence; that is, into nations, cities, towns, countryside, neighbourhoods.
2. Sexual division of labour; that is, that differential allocation of gender into spheres of production/reproduction, and the organisation of sexual relations.
3. Religious/ethnic/racial allocation of subjects.
4. Differentiation of subjects on the basis of trade-union and professional associations, artistic and leisure organisations, political parties, media institutions, etc.
5. Generational allocation of subjects. (Urry, 1981: 70)

The organisations discussed in this chapter can be categorised according to this hierarchy. For example, the Country Women's Association of New South Wales has stood firmly by its conception of rurality, which has a strongly spatial element, and has fought for improved conditions of health, education and transport for country residents. In terms of *gender roles,* it has accepted a primarily domestic role for women, and has attempted to make this role less onerous while broadening women's horizons. It has never challenged the rigid separation of gender roles in rural New South Wales, nor seriously attempted to project an image of women as farmers, either in their own right or as partners in the family farm, despite the fact that some of its members do fulful such roles. In *ethnic terms,* the Country Women's Association speaks firmly in support of the British heritage of the Australian nation rather than its multicultural character. In *politics,* it is acknowledged as sympathetic to right-wing parties. As far as *generation* is concerned, it is decreasingly representative of rural women as a whole because of the ageing of its membership.

'Spatiality', argues Soja, 'must be socially *reproduced,* and this reproduction process presents a continuing source of struggle, conflict and contradiction' (Soja, 1985: 97). The particular arena of situated social struggle in which rural women's networks play their part comprises the countryside and its rural society. But these are notoriously difficult terms to define. Williams (1985) investigates the perceived opposition of *The Country and the City* in his book of that title. However, in his discussion of the term 'country' (Williams, 1985: 307) he does not mention the meaning of country as 'nation', which is a crucial and politically exploited ambiguity in Australia's history. The Country Parties (independent Country Parties existed in all states by the late 1920s as well as a Federal Country Party) and the Country Women's Association have all used the term 'country' to invoke a patriotic ideology aimed at transcending city/country divisions, and asserting the country as the heartland of the nation and its values. The Country Women's Association's motto begins: 'Honour to God, Loyalty to the Throne, Service to the Country'. Although its members understand 'Country' to mean 'rural Australia', the political party with which they have always been closely affiliated, the right-wing Country Party, has changed its name – significantly – to the National Party, although its supporters are overwhelmingly non-metropolitan.

Addressing the question of whether such a thing as rural society exists, Mormont concludes that 'the rural is a category of thought', . . . 'a constructed representation and not an ascertained reality' (Mormont, 1990: 22, 40 and 41). Most of the traditional women's networks discussed here now have branches and a significant membership in urban locations, reflecting not only the broadening of their original objectives, but also the migration of rural women to the towns and cities, and the spread of urban areas which have engulfed many former rural localities where branches existed. It is the newer, non-traditional networks that are today firmly based in agricultural areas, reflecting their narrower agenda, which, in the case of the Ontario Farm Women's Network and of Women in Agriculture (New Zealand), is focused on women on the farm. It is these newer networks that are attempting to redefine those aspects of gender relations that have been identified with rurality in the past and that in many rural localities persist strongly, subordinating and even exploiting women (Dempsey, 1992). Here, the 'situated social struggle' is focused on gender relations.

In Australia, especially inland, there is a much clearer demarcation of urban from rural areas than in Europe or eastern Ontario, and it would be harder to assert that 'the opposition between town and country has hardly any social meaning for the majority of inhabitants' (Mormont, 1990: 38). Apart from those favoured coastal areas still attracting population growth, there is a fiercely asserted perception of the difference of country values from city values – a perception that has scarcely changed since the 1920s, and that is characterised by Mormont's 'common properties' of 'rural societies': small-scale communities (often, in Australia, characterised by very low population densities), conscious of their history (recent though it may be by European standards, as much of the inland has only been settled by non-Aborigines for a century and a half at most), and with strong local economic and social cohesion among the settlers. But, as Mormont points out, there are powerful developments that render this consciousness of difference a defensive strategy against the demands of non-local agents seeking to use the country for recreation, waste disposal, water supply, second homes, retirement and so on; and the rural population itself is highly mobile and often educated in the cities. The permeability of contemporary rural communities is demonstrated by the fact that the newer rural women's networks are strongly influenced by the feminist movement that has its firm base in the cities, a movement which, in general, is neither understood nor supported by traditional rural women's organisations.

The deeply conservative attitude to gender relations that typifies Australian rural communities – including country towns – is an integral part of their contemporary social identity. Mormont does not mention this as a significant, distinguishing characteristic of rurality. It is unlikely that this is a characteristic peculiar to rural Australia. The gender order of Australian society as a whole is characterised by male hegemony which is expressed in its most extreme form in the specific gender regime of rural communities. Referring particularly to rural Victoria, Dempsey describes gender relations as 'a system of male superordination and female subordination and, at times, exploitation' (Dempsey, 1992: 3; see also Poiner, 1990; Alston, 1990). Traditional research into social networks has identified 'marked conjugal separation' as characteristic of interaction in rural contexts (Bott, 1971: 251). Bott's work indicated that in close-knit social networks there appeared at that time to be 'a sharp cleavage by sex' (Fallding, quoted by Bott, 1971: 242). As rural communities are characterised by close-knit social networks, the fact that many organised groups in rural areas are organised on gender lines is not, therefore, surprising. Dempsey's work confirms the persistence of the separate social spheres of women and men in rural Australia. Poiner identifies women in rural NSW as supporting male hegemony, partly because of the legitimisation this hegemony is given by tradition. Alston (1990) suggests that the only source of power and prestige for women on Australian family farms lies in their traditional, lynchpin role carrying out tasks many of which are at one and the same time productive and reproductive. Loss of this role would leave them marginalised in rural communities, and therefore they affirm it strongly.

The term 'network' does not have a precise and generally accepted meaning (Bott, 1971: 314–30). It is, however, a useful concept, and its implications can be briefly outlined. Social networks have spatial and temporal dimensions. They comprise nodes, links between them and the transfer of information between the nodes via the links. The information exchange may take place in a particular locality at a pre-arranged time, may be transmitted sporadically, or on a more or less continuous basis, with the network always in place and ready to be activated. There may be face-to-face contact and/or other means of communication e.g. letters or a variety of electronic means. A network may be formally or loosely structured, or consist of unstructured contacts united by a shared interest. Single events can be important catalysts for personal development, policy-making or concerted action by members of the network. Networks are selective, and just as significant as those *included* are those *excluded*.

The close-knit nature of the various networks in rural areas needs emphasising (Barnes, 1954; Bott, 1971). Many people in rural communities have friends in common. In rural NSW, individuals may have extended kin networks both within their neighbourhood and also spread thinly over the vast, lightly populated interior of the state. Distance does not attenuate the power of such networks. The 'three regions or fields in the social system' (based on territory, industry/occupation/and friendship/kin) of the Norwegian village studied by Barnes (1954: 42) all overlap, so that an individual's 'interactional matrix' (Bott, 1971: 322) comprises many and intersecting social networks, which Boissevain (1974: 28) refers to as 'multiplex'. To select out certain organisations, as in this chapter, is to examine only one part of the complex pattern of social interaction in rural areas.

Clearly, networks have spatial dimensions, but they have important temporal dimensions too. Particular organisations are established in response to a perceived need. After periods of growth they can decay, atrophy and even be closed down. Hence, they are themselves outcomes of the structuration process. But also, through the passing on to new members and to the next generation of certain values, memories and particular sub-cultures, rural women's organisations are significant agents in the structuration process. 'The structuring of space is inseparable from the process of social structuring' (Pred, 1986: 5). To conclude, rural women's organisations are agencies involved in 'socially produc[ing] space'. In Soja's terms they are both a 'medium' and an 'outcome of social action and relationship'. Not only are they a means of coping with people's dispersal throughout space, but also, as will be discussed, once established, they have the power to transform aspects of the perceptions of their members and of those of the community as a whole. This is particularly significant, as such networks encapsulate all three dimensions of Soja's concept of spatiality: socially produced space, physical space and mental space. Rural women's networks, then, integrate members who are at a distance from each other, facilitate action, develop a sense of shared values, achievement and history, and permit an on-going identification and evaluation of issues significant to women in the context of rurality. They reflect, in part, a response to people's dispersal in physical space; shape the perceptions both of those involved and of those who observe their operations and are implicated in the social reproduction and transformation of rurality.

Rural women's organisations in action

The rest of this chapter will concentrate on organisations purposefully set up by, or for, women in rural areas in Australia, New Zealand, Britain and Canada. As will be seen, some such organisations are long-established, e.g. the National Federation of Women's Institutes in Britain (NFWI) and the Country Women's Association of New South Wales, Australia (CWA). These have become part of their nation's popular culture; they tend to be conservative in outlook and to reinforce traditional ideologies and social structures. Other newer organisations, such as the Ontario Farm Women's Network (OFWN), challenge such ideologies and structures and represent part of the on-going struggle in society at large to transform gender relations. Both types of organisation are gender based, not only in restricting membership to women, but also in reflecting an agenda of women's interests separate from those of men. However, the objectives of the two types of organisation differ significantly. Whereas the more radical OFWN was established with a prime objective of challenging power relations in rural communities on both the personal and the institutional level, the older organisations do not make it a major policy objective to change gender relations nor to challenge male hegemony. Some of the older organisations, faced with static or declining membership, are modifying their missions, activities and subcultures in order to appeal to new potential members, but their strategy, rather than becoming more radical, is to broaden their focus to address issues relating to the family or the rural community as a whole rather than to women specifically. For example, in New Zealand, Women's Division, Federated Farmers (WDFF) have recently adopted as their mission statement: 'To strengthen rural communities in New Zealand', whereas their prime object remains, as it has been for 72 years, 'To better the conditions of women and children living in the country' (WDFF, 1991: 6).

Formal structures typify traditional women's organisations like the NFWI and the CWA. An appropriate concept is one of layers of nodes and links. Each layer is superimposed on another with the largest number of nodes in the base layer and a single node at the top representing the head office or equivalent. The CWA consists of two sets of such networks organised on a regional basis but with, at a third level, a single head office. CWA organisations in other Australian states represent quite discrete sets with their own state headquarters. Internationally, well over 2 million members of 247 constituent and associate organisations of rural women in over 70 countries, including many in the South, liaise regularly as the Associated Country Women of the World (ACWW – Buff, 1992: 11).

In contrast, some of the rural women's organisations established in the last few years may be structured quite differently (e.g. the Rural Women's Network, Victoria, Australia – RWN – discussed below), often in reaction to what members perceive as masculinist, rigid and autocratic structures of decision-making. They are clearly influenced by second-wave feminism, which 'employed informal, participatory and consensual organisational styles' (Sawer and Simms, 1984: 99). As yet their geographic fields are more limited than the traditional organisations and there is no international 'umbrella' structure comparable with the ACWW, although links between them are currently being developed. At present, there are some significant rural women's movements that are more 'states of mind' than organisations, such as the New Zealand's Women in Agriculture and the informal – but increasingly structured – networking behind the Rural Women's Conferences/Gatherings/Speakouts in Australia. It seems that, where powerful and traditional social structures are being challenged for the first time, as in agricultural communities, women are still experimenting with appropriate ways of focusing energies especially when numbers involved in the challenge are relatively small. Sporadic bursts of effort, as when a conference or 'speak-out' is organised, may be all that is possible at present.

Both traditional and non-traditional women's organisations mediate between broad social structures and the everyday activities of members. As

Figure 2.1 Contrasting organisational structures of CWA of New South Wales and OFWN

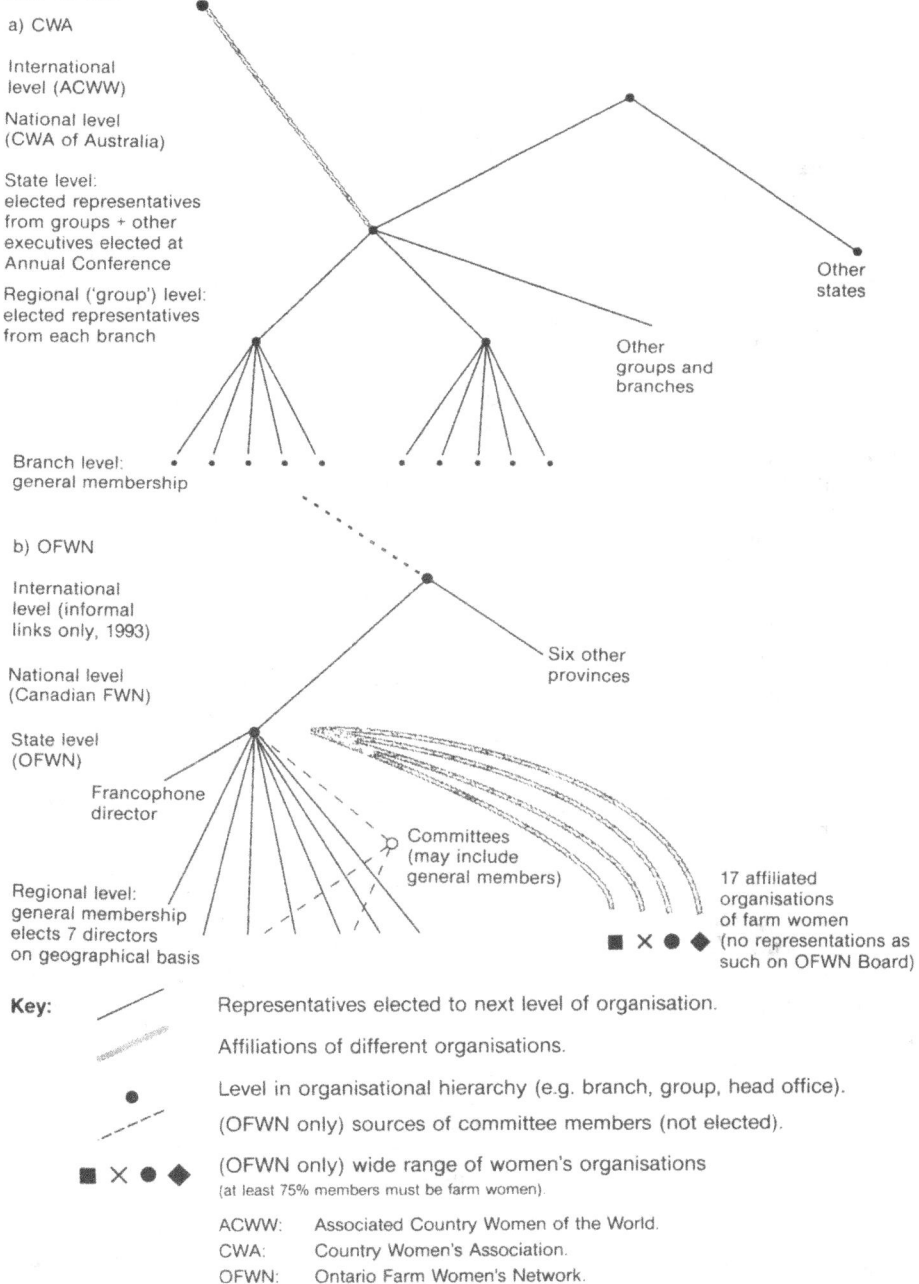

a) CWA

International
level (ACWW)

National level
(CWA of Australia)

State level:
elected representatives
from groups + other
executives elected at
Annual Conference

Regional ('group') level:
elected representatives
from each branch

Other
states

Other
groups and
branches

Branch level:
general membership

b) OFWN

International
level (informal
links only, 1993)

Six other
provinces

National level
(Canadian FWN)

State level
(OFWN)

Francophone
director

Committees
(may include
general members)

17 affiliated
organisations
of farm women
(no representations as
such on OFWN Board)

Regional level:
general membership
elects 7 directors
on geographical basis

Key:

Representatives elected to next level of organisation.

Affiliations of different organisations.

Level in organisational hierarchy (e.g. branch, group, head office).

(OFWN only) sources of committee members (not elected).

(OFWN only) wide range of women's organisations
(at least 75% members must be farm women).

ACWW: Associated Country Women of the World.
CWA: Country Women's Association.
OFWN: Ontario Farm Women's Network.

traditional rural women's networks are having difficulty in recruiting new members, it would appear that they are no longer addressing issues of prime concern to younger women. The NFWI in England is currently asking members for help in refining the organisation's role and purpose. The WDFF commissioned a report on its future in 1984–5, and among one of the consultant's preliminary comments was the statement: 'To remain relevant to the needs of the changing society organisational goals and policies must therefore always be subject to constant review. The alternative is to risk obsolescence and eventual decline and decay' (Williams, quoted in Luxton, 1985: 59). However, organisations that have stood firmly by traditional ideologies may find that the upheaval of such review is too challenging to the structures that lie at the heart of their identity and rationality (Teather, 1992a). For example, as Whatmore (1991) found for farming women in England, many farm women see themselves primarily as the channel through which a farm may pass to their sons, and are committed to the continuation of the family farm as a business, even if their own non-farm earnings are the crutch that keeps it from financial collapse. Many are deeply involved in the maintenance of kinship and community networks which effectively perpetuate current patterns of patriarchal gender relations (see for example Moyal, 1992: Poiner, 1990; and Encel et al., 1974). However, current research in Australia indicates that farm women 'are actively encouraging their children away from farming' and that many find intense stress in family farm kinship relationships (Alston, on-going and 1992: 19). The CWA, devoted wholeheartedly for three generations to transmitting an ideology that secured the economic and social status quo and sited women's and children's needs within it, can no longer do so effectively because of its failure to recruit young women. It might be expected that the significance of the CWA as an agency shaping rurality would therefore be reduced. Instead, its prestige and influence remain high, partly because it has no competitors as a representative of rural women in the state and partly because of its long-established lines of consultation with government bureaucracies.

Equally, however, their hostility to social groups and ideas that challenge these traditional values, and the rural communities that they are seen to underpin, is shared by many rural women and traditional women's networks in Canada, New Zealand and elsewhere. Such challenges come from those who call for greater recognition of social problems (such as domestic violence) which challenge the uniformly neighbourly and harmonious image of rural communities, from women calling for fairer allocation of marital assets, involving farm assets, on the breakup of marriage; from women with sceptical attitudes to marriage; from women challenging institutionalised heterosexuality and masculinity (see Middleton, 1986, for an account of her experience in an English rural community), and from women seeking to break into or improve their status in professions related to the agricultural sector.

Traditional rural women's networks have centred their missions around a concept of rurality that is perceived as sharply differentiated from urban, particularly metropolitan, ways of life and value systems (epitomised by the 'countrymindedness' ideology of NSW – Aitkin, 1985); around the concept of the nuclear family (or two or three generation farm family); and around a system of patriarchal gender relations that subordinates women. Each of these three concepts – rurality, the nuclear family and patriarchal gender relations – is undergoing fundamental change in Western societies. That the long-term survival of organisations such as the CWA is in doubt is largely because of the members' reluctance to acknowledge the processes of change that are under-way and to adjust their mission and modes of operating to reflect them. There is a disjunction with broader social structures; a failure of the organisations as agents to mediate between dominant social trends and the sectors of society that they represent; an attempt to resist economic and social transformations that impinge on rural women. The values, publications, buildings and patterns of interaction typical of such organisations represent both a concrete and an abstract 'sedimentation' of ideologies that were dominant in a past period. The contrast between two specific rural women's organisations – a traditional and a radical one – will be the focus of the next two sections.

Traditional rural women's networks: the Country Women's Association of New South Wales, Australia

The Country Women's Association of New South Wales was founded in 1922 (Townsend, 1988; Teather, 1992a, b; 1993, 1994). Each state in Australia has its own, independent CWA. In this chapter the abbreviation CWA refers specifically to the CWA of NSW. In 1991, the CWA had about 16,000 members (less than half the peak in the 1950s) and just over 500 branches covering the whole of the state. Until recently the largest women's organisation in NSW, the CWA is part of the state's popular culture. Its primary mission is 'To improve the welfare and conditions of women and children in the country'. It is recognised by all political parties as the voice of rural women, and has a consultative role on many official bodies. No other organisation exists that can claim to speak for rural women. It should be pointed out, however, that the CWA has a very high proportion of elderly members and a large proportion live not on rural properties and farms but in country towns, metropolitan and metropolitan fringe areas.

Similar organisations exist in other Western countries, e.g. the Federated Women's Institutes of Canada (FWIC – membership 32,933, 1991), founded in Ontario in 1897; the National Federation of Women's Institutes in Britain (membership 310,000, 1992), originally founded in Wales by a Canadian woman in 1915; the Country Women's Institutes of New Zealand (NZCWI – 19,800 members, 1992), founded in 1921 by a woman inspired by the English example; and New Zealand's Women's Division Federated Farmers (WDFF – 7,642 members, 1991), founded in 1925 (information from annual reports or executives of organisations mentioned, and Luxton, 1985; Harper, n.d.). It is usual for such organisations to be non-party political. There may well have been an unacknowledged, but subsidiary, political agenda behind the establish-ment of the CWA (Teather, 1994).

The rise of the CWA in the 1920s and 1930s represented a form of social and spatial organisation facilitated by the technological improvements and innovations of the time (e.g. the telephone and the private motor car) as well as by social progress (e.g. improving standards of literacy and the extension of the vote to women before the First World War). The CWA was also driven by rising expectations (e.g. the desire for better health care and the rejection of the privations of rural life). After 1922, women who joined the CWA gained an unprecedented sense of commitment to each other, to their shared concerns and to their state-wide organisation through the shared experience of local fund-raising activities, the property purchased by the branch, and the various activities throughout the year on a regional or state-wide basis that brought delegates from different branches together. It is important to recognise the isolation in which some of these women lived, particularly in that part of the state west of the Great Divide. A visit to the local town before the Second World War might involve a matter of hours in a buggy on unsealed roads impassable after rains, and might only take place every few weeks or less.

The CWA probably transformed its members' perceptions of space. It did this in four ways. Firstly, rural and urban women were linked together and learnt of each other's shared and differing concerns. Secondly, members' world views were extended beyond the local. Thirdly, in a country woman's home territory, a CWA member had, for the first time in rural NSW towns, a public space that was legitimately hers – the CWA Rest Room. Finally, women could assess the problems inherent in their living environments in the confidence that there existed an organisation specifically set up to identify and address the needs of women and children in rural areas.

Like other traditional rural women's organisations, the CWA has been a very significant political agent throughout much of its existence. The CWA has fought attempts by male politicians to overlook, marginalise or depoliticise social reproductive issues of central importance to women's lives. In view of the patriarchal attitudes to women that have prevailed during this century, it has chosen to operate as a quietly assertive lobby group, using family connections (husbands and fathers especially) to gain access to politicians. This conservative mode of operation made considerable strides in achieving better services for women and children in rural areas in NSW in the first decades of the CWA (Townsend, 1988).

A significant aspect of such traditional organisations in the structuration process is to have clarified such concepts as 'rurality' and 'countrymindedness' (Aitkin, 1985). They have also stood firmly by the very concepts that non-traditional rural women's organisations are determined to transform: patriarchal gender relations in rural areas and in the agricultural industry, and the concept of a nuclear family where the role of women is as a 'helpmate' – an auxiliary rather than equal partner. The CWA's rural vision represents a form of spatiality produced in response to particular conditions and which transformed women's cognition of space in the 1920s and 1930s. It is a striking example of the potential power of networks as collective agencies in the structuration process.

Non-traditional rural women's networks: the Ontario Farm Women's Network, Canada

The OFWN represents a more radical rural women's organisation; one of 41 non-traditional networks throughout Canada (Harkin, 1991). In Ontario, as well as the OFWN, there is Women for the Survival of Agriculture (WSA); another, Concerned Farm Women, existed from 1981–90. Whereas traditional rural women's organisations have never focused exclusively on farm women, these newer ones do precisely that. This parallels the tendency of research, in which: '[t]he study of the agricultural has become divorced from the rural' (Marsden *et al.*, 1990: 6). The agenda of farm women is quite separate from the broader agenda of female rural residents, many of whom, today, may have nothing to do with the agricultural sector.

Members of such organisations as the OFWN see farm women as businesswomen whose priority is to run profitable enterprises using the most up-to-date techniques. However, the commitment of members of these newer organisations to the survival of the family farm and to the farming way of life is not in question. The challenge they make is to the gender-role ideologies that have traditionally underpinned that way of life. Such organisations are undertaking the mediating role between rural women and wider developments, in terms of women's emancipation, that has been eschewed by traditional rural women's organisations. As Harkin (1991: 2) puts it:

> By [1975–80], more and more farm women who had been content to retain the values and traditions of rural life, to carry on their roles as wife, mother, homemaker, farm worker and manager and often off-farm employee, began to share the anxiety, concern and even anger expressed by women in the early ranks of the new farm women's movement.

The differing agendas of traditional and non-traditional rural women's networks meant that hostility between the two was inevitable in Canada in the 1970s (Harkin, 1991), and regrets remain that the FWIO has not become the vehicle through which more radical women press their agenda. It is interesting to note that the FWIO has recently set up its own Farm Women's Advisory Committees.

Apart from fundamental differences in ideology from the older rural women's organisations, the newer ones have a different network structure. It is too early to comment on the temporal dimensions of these rural women's organisations, but in an era of rapid social, economic and technological change it is unlikely that they will be as enduring as the traditional organisations. Certainly they have not grown so fast as, for example, the CWA or the FWIC did in their early years. In New South Wales, the CWA had 120 branches and 4,500 members within its first five (Townsend, 1988: 15); throughout Canada, the FWIC had 892 branches and nearly 30,000 members after 20 years (Ambrose, 1989: 7). The OFWN had 310 individual members in 1991 and 15 affiliated organisations after three years of existence; WSA has 1,200 members after 16 years (Farm Women's Bureau, 1991). Despite their small size, it would seem that efficient use of lobbying and the media has enabled these networks to make significant progress towards achieving their goals (Harkin, 1991). Conferences are a crucial element of the new networks. The first National Farm Women's Conference in Canada was held in 1980; subsequent ones were held in 1985, 1987, 1989 and 1991.

The small size, proliferation and lack of an over-arching organisational structure of non-traditional rural women's networks in Canada, reflects the totally different physical, social and mental dimensions of space in the late, compared with the early, twentieth century. The greater opportunities for consultation, electronically or face to face, in contemporary Canada, mean that rigid managerial structures can readily be subverted. It is less easy for higher levels of a network to insist on members and branches keeping to an agreed agenda. Ease of communication is in sympathy with the late-twentieth-century intolerance of autocratic processes. Fragmentation of an interest group into factions is all too frequent. This may be one reason underlying the failure of newer rural women's networks to form cohesive, expanding organisations as did their traditional predecessors. Paradoxically, greater ease of communication has the power to generate not only greater unity but also enhanced awareness of regional and other differences and a greater desire to affirm these.

In New South Wales, there are as yet no new rural women's organisations similar to those in Canada, but three Rural Women's Conferences have been held, in 1991, 1992 and 1993. They were called, significantly, not by 'grass-roots' movements but by government agencies – the NSW government's advisory body, known as the Women's Advisory Council, and the Rural Women's Network Co-ordinator (the latter appointed by the state government in 1991). In Victoria, Australia, the two paid members of the state-wide Rural Women's Network assisted farm women to set up Women in Agriculture Inc. in 1993. This, like the CWA seventy years earlier, has been inspired by Canadian examples and had 250 members in early 1993.

The new networks are not accompanied by significant changes in perceptions of space, as were the older networks. The significance of the newer networks is twofold. First, they are agents in transforming women's attitudes to their place in rural society – places that are very different from those of rural women in the past. It is not isolation and loneliness – which relate to the physical dimensions of space – that the newer rural women's organisations are combatting, but attitudes towards women's social position that members perceive as inappropriate and inequitable. In other words, these newer organisations are committed to transforming the mental and cognitive attitudes of rural people. With a powerful traditional rural ideology militating against the aspirations of such women, networking is an essential weapon to maintain commitment and morale. Non-traditional women's organisations focus on asserting a new concept of farm women's roles and on transforming attitudes to farm women on the local scale (e.g. in daily interactions between farm women and men who are employed in agricultural service industries) and at the state and federal level (e.g. in attaining female representation on agricultural boards). Details of the overwhelming male domination of such boards in New Zealand and Canada are provided in reports by the New Zealand Ministry of Agriculture (1992) and the Farm Women's Bureau (1991).

Secondly, rural women who participate in non-traditional organisations have moved well beyond the efforts of their grandmothers in the 1920s and 1930s to establish spaces for women and children on the streets of country towns – rest rooms and baby health centres. They are asserting their right to a seat in the board room. Both planks of the agenda represent fundamental aspects of the gender struggle throughout Western society. The confrontation between traditional and non-traditional rural women's organisations is at the heart of the on-going restructuring of rural communities.

Conclusions

Rural women's organisations have for decades challenged, and continue to challenge and redefine, concepts of rurality. The non-traditional organisations are currently tackling gender issues at the local level – that of farm women subjected daily to discriminatory attitudes, for example from employees of agricultural service industries. The family farm is the workplace of these women, where their productive and reproductive roles are closely, even inseparably, linked. To establish an organisation that brings farm women into regular contact so that experiences can be compared and evaluated, individual determination strengthened, and collective policies adopted, is following the traditions of women's political action this century. It is a bottom-up process not led, but sometimes assisted, by women with positions in government bureaucracy. Women with no experience of formal politics are, through non-traditional rural women's organisations, learning skills that are essentially political: persuading others on a personal and public level of the legitimacy of their point of view, using the media, organising lobbying activities and so on. They are acutely aware that 'formal political equality is of little value to women in the absence of changes in gender relations' (Stacey and Price, quoted in Bondi and Peake, 1988: 35).

Giddens argues that daily activities have a recursive influence on pervasive and long-established social structures. Non-traditional rural women's organisations are attempting to subvert the rules that have conventionally set limits to behaviour and dominated attitudes. Thus, they assert that a farmer can be female, with all that this assumption implies. The irony is that farm women have always been farmers. Now they are learning to be more effective at saying so. These new networks are efficient ways of challenging social structures and of altering stubbornly held perceptions and attitudes. The 'mental space of cognition and representation' relating to rurality is a central target for non-traditional rural women's organisations. The entrenched sexism of rural communities means that individual women need to network in order to gain confidence, establish a strong public profile and maintain their determination.

Traditional rural women's organisations provide useful precedents and even models for today's networks. The CWA and the FWIO, for example, became, and remain, formidable and effective lobbyists. They strove for what is, arguably, the necessary first stage in women's emancipation: the facilities that help them carry out their reproductive role efficiently, with confidence and without jeopardising their health. Furthermore, these early, gendered networks, and the spaces owned and managed by women, permitted new forms of awareness to develop elsewhere.

> This goal of a society in which freedom and participation of one group is not won at the expense of others can only be realised by eliminating the inequalities of power between men and women. The patriarchal power structures, however, are so deeply ingrained in all spheres of life that women need space to establish their own conditions and priorities, in order to determine how they can assert control over their social, as well as their private, life. (Ter Veld, 1992: 7 (ACWW Triennial Conference, 1992))

Non-traditional rural women's organisations represent the generation that has emerged from this strategy and is now asserting its right to a share in the control of agricultural business and professional spheres. The older organisations have shown themselves unable to incorporate such aims into their missions. Newer organisations can only seek their sympathy and support, as has been done in Victoria, Australia, where the International President of the ACWW, a long-time member of the CWA of Victoria, is to be Patron of Women in Agriculture's international conference in 1994.

This chapter has not attempted to cover, in a comprehensive manner, all types of women's networks operating in rural areas. Instead, it has concentrated on examples of rural women's networks from a number of developed countries, and has argued that such networks have been significant agents for change. Such organisations illustrate the partial truth that 'the home and the community as workplaces become the locus of political activity arising from issues of "reproduction" in a manner parallel to the shopfloor in connection with production issues' (Bondi and Peake, 1988: 36). However, the agenda of farm women is not limited to reproductive issues. The farm is a home *and* a work place, the locus of productive *and* reproductive activities. There is no separation of public and private spheres for farm women and the personal is of intense political significance to them as they attempt to restructure gender relations in rural areas. Today, certain newer rural women's organisations are challenging the nature of gender relations in the context of the agricultural industry and in associated local communities. A particular form of feminism – 'bush feminism' – is developing that is tailored to rural society and focused on the farm sector. Recently established rural women's networks, therefore, contribute to the (re)construction, or continuing structuration, of rurality. Members of these networks have firmly established gender relations as an issue to be contested in the rural arena – an arena which, up till recently, has been a safe refuge for patriarchy. Conversely, the perception and experience of rurality is undergoing challenge and change as women, particularly those on farms, seek a more equitable share in all aspects of decision-making and a more accurate definition, and wider understanding, of their role in rural communities.

The concept of rurality requires continuous revision and redefinition as part of the endless transformation of the woven cloth of society. Women's networking – their pattern of linked threads in this cloth – is a complex and varied process. It is a long-established, dynamic element of rural society, highly significant at both the local and the state or national level. Through networking, women have gained power as social agents and been able to inscribe new patterns of interaction and organisation on the mental and social spaces that contribute to concepts of rurality.

Acknowledgements

The comments of Associate Professors D.J. Walmsley and J.H. Bell, University of New England, and of Dr Sarah Whatmore, University of Bristol, have been particularly helpful to me in the preparation of this chapter. I am grateful to Mrs A. Gillman (NFWI branch executive member), to Mrs Joan Barham, Guelph, Ontario, and to executives of the WDFF, NZCWI and NZ Ministry of Agriculture, who have supplied information.

References

Aitkin, D. (1985) 'Countrymindedness' – the spread of an idea. *Australian Cultural History*, 4: 34–41.

Alston, M. (1990) Feminism and farm women. *Australian Social Work*, 43: 23–7.

Alston, M. (1992) Socio-cultural factors affecting farm ownership. In Lees, J., *Family Farm Book*. University of New England, Armidale, NSW 2351, Rural Development Centre (unpublished).

Ambrose, L.M. (1989) Women's Institute: on the fringe of women's history. *Past and Present*, February: 7–9.

Barnes, J.A. (1954) Class and committees in a Norwegian island parish. *Human Relations*, 7(1): 39–58.

Boissevain, J. (1974) *Friends of Friends. Networks, Manipulators and Coalitions*. Oxford, Basil Blackwell.

Bondi, L. and Peake, L. (1988) Gender and the city: urban politics revisited. In Little, J., Peake, L. and Richardson, P., *Women in Cities*. Houndmills, Basingstoke, Macmillan Education.

Bott, E. (1971) *Family and Social Network*. London, Tavistock Publications.

Buff, B. (1992) Conference business. *Countrywoman*, October–December: 11.

Dempsey, K. (1990) *Smalltown. A Study of Social Inequality, Cohesion and Belonging*. Melbourne, Oxford University Press.

Dempsey, K. (1992) *A Man's Town. Inequality Between Women and Men in Rural Australia*. Melbourne, Oxford University Press.

Encel, S., MacKenzie, N. and Tebbutt, M. (1974) *Women and Society: An Australian Study*. Melbourne, Cheshire.

Farm Women's Bureau/Bureau des agricultrices (1991) *Fact Sheets: Farm Women's Organizations, Canada, 1991*. Sir John Carling Building, Ottawa, Ontario K1A 0C5, Agriculture Canada.

Fitchen, J.M. (1991) *Endangered Spaces. Enduring Places: Change, Identity and Survival in Rural America.* Boulder, Westview Press.

Haralambos, M. (1990) *Sociology. Themes and Perspectives.* 3rd edition. London, Unwin Hyman.

Harkin, D. (1991) A summary history of the new Farm Women's Movement, in Farm Women's Bureau/Bureau des agricultrices. *Fact Sheets: Farm Women's Organizations, Canada, 1991,* 1–4. Sir John Carling Building, Ottawa, Ontario K1A 0C5, Agriculture Canada.

Harper, B. (n.d., c. 1959) *History of the Country Women's Institutes of New Zealand 1921–1958.* (Probably Wellington), Whitcombe and Tombs.

Lawrence, G. (1990) Agricultural restructuring and rural social change in Australia. In Marsden, T., Lowe, P. and Whatmore, S. (eds), *Rural Restructuring, Global Processes and their Responses, Critical Perspectives in Rural Change Series:* 101–27. London, David Fulton.

Luxton, T. (1985) *In Community of Spirit. A History of the Women's Division, Federated Farmers of New Zealand,* Auckland West, Lindon.

Marsden, T., Lowe, P. and Whatmore, S. (1990) Introduction: questions of rurality. In Marsden, T., Lowe, P. and Whatmore, S. (eds) *Rural Restructuring, Global Processes and their Responses, Critical Perspectives in Rural Change Series:* 1–20. London, David Fulton.

Middleton, A. (1986) Marking boundaries: men's space and women's space in a Yorkshire village. In Lowe, P., Bradley, T. and Wright, S. (eds), *Deprivation and Welfare in Rural Areas:* 121–34. Norwich, Geobooks.

Mitchell, J. (1992) When you're 50k out. In Franklin, M-A. Short, L. and Teather, E.K. (eds), *Country Women at the Crossroads.* University of New England, Armidale NSW 2351, Department of Sociology (unpublished).

Mormont, M. (1990) Who is rural? Or how to be rural: towards a sociology of the rural. In Marsden, T., Lowe, P. and Whatmore, S. (eds), *Rural Restructuring, Global Processes and their Responses:* 21–45. London, David Fulton.

Moyal, A. (1992) Women and telecommunications in Australia. Pointers to a research field. Paper delivered at the *Australian Historical Society Conference,* Canberra, October.

New Zealand Ministry of Agriculture (1992) *The Contribution of Agriculture to the Rural Economy, Stage One: Scoping Report. MAF Policy Technical Paper 92/4.* Wellington, NZ, Ministry of Agriculture.

Pioner, G. (1990) *The Good Old Rule. Gender and Other Power Relationships in a Rural Community.* Sydney, Sydney University Press.

Pred, A. (1986) *Place, Practice and Structure.* Cambridge, Polity.

Roberts, B. (1992) Women in rural conservation and landcare. In Franklin, M-A., Short, L. and Teather, E.K. (eds), *Country Women at the Crossroads.* University of New England, Armidale, NSW 2351, Department of Sociology (in press).

Sawer, M. and Simms, M. (1984) *A Woman's Place. Women and Politics in Australia.* Sydney, Allen and Unwin.

Soja, E.W. (1985) The spatiality of social life: towards a transformative retheorisation. In Gregory, D. and Urry, J. *Social Relations and Spatial Structures:* 90–127. Basingstoke, Macmillan.

Taylor, M. (1991) Economic restructuring and regional change in Australia. *Australian Geographical Studies,* 29(2): 255–67.

Teather, E.K. (1992a) Remote rural women's ideologies, spaces and networks: the example of the Country Women's Association of New South Wales, 1922–1992. *Australian and New Zealand Journal of Sociology,* 28(3): 369–90.

Teather, E.K. (1992b) The first rural women's network in NSW: seventy years of the Country Women's Association. *Australian Geographer,* 23(2): 164–76.

Teather, E.K. (1993) The past and present mandate of the Country Women's Assocition, paper presented at Conference on Interest Groups and Political Lobbying, Politics Department, University of New England, June 1993.

Teather, E.K. (in press 1994) The CWA as a counter-revolutionary organisation. *Australian Cultural Studies,* 40 or 42.

Ter Veld, E. (1992), Women's agenda for the future, *Countrywoman,* October–December: 7–8.

Townsend, H. (1988) *Serving the Country.* Sydney, Doubleday.

Urry, J. (1981) *The Anatomy of Capitalist Societies. The Economy, Civil Society and the State.* London, Macmillan.

Whatmore, S. (1991) *Farming Women. Gender, Work and Family Enterprise.* Basingstoke, Macmillan.

Williams, R. (1985) *The Country and the City.* London, Hogarth Press.

Women's Division, Federated Farmers (1991) WDFF Strategic Plan. *Rural Woman,* November–December: 6.

CHAPTER 3

Constructing the Future: Cooperation and Resistance Among Farm Women in Ireland[1]

Patricia O'Hara

Introduction

In Ireland family farming as a social form has immense economic, social and ideological significance. Indeed the Irish Constitution obliges the state to ensure that as many 'families' as possible be retained on the land.[2] The 'family farm' remains the typical agricultural production unit.[3] Although the number of people who classify themselves occupationally as farmers has been declining throughout this century, there is little evidence of significant consolidation of landholdings or the emergence of a class of capitalist farmers. Agrarian restructuring over the past few decades has been characterised by concentration of production on the larger more commercialised farms so that a decreasing share of total agricultural output and income comes from smaller holdings. On these, earnings from off-farm work have been crucial for the persistence of family farming. Family members have been particularly adapt at capturing such limited employment opportunities as existed in rural areas. Either spouse may be working off the farm but the generation of off-farm income is critical to the family's livelihood and allows family farming to survive (Hannan and Commins, 1992).

The family farm is treated as a unity in agricultural discourse, in official statistics and by farming organisations and agribusiness. Policy debates about the changing nature of agrarian structures, how family farming should be supported, the significance of pluriactivity, farm diversification and so on, are

50

based on implicit assumptions about the family farm and the 'farm family', assuming a unity of interests among its members. Farm women rarely feature in this discourse. The official and public face of family farming in Ireland is that of the farmer – usually male – who owns the land, represents the family in farming organisations, is subject to taxation or entitled to social security. The occupation and work of 'farmers' and other relatives are included in official statistics but not the work of farm wives/mothers. The invisbility of women's work and their lack of professional status is underpinned by the patrilineal system of farm inheritance so that most women enter farming through marriage or become farmers by being widowed. Farm women's status and entitlement from farming usually derive from their relationship to male 'farmers'. Women on family farms are thus in a structurally unequal situation to men, so they cannot be assumed to have the same interests. Yet they are at the heart of family farming because its existence is dependent on family formation, development and reproduction – processes which intimately involve women.

The conditions of agricultural restructuring indicate that farm families are not just adapting in a defensive way to external forces but are also seizing opportunities afforded by wider structural trends (in the labour market, for instance) and are thereby active agents in the process of change. In this chapter it is argued that farm women can have a separate and distinct influence on both the nature and the continuity of family farming. Their subordinate position on family farms has given rise to particular strategies – cooperation and resistance – which structure family farming and its future. The assumption of the unified farm family obscures not only women's subordination, but also their responses to it. Women are not as powerless as they might appear. They have always contested patriarchal structures, most visibly by avoiding marriage to farmers in the first place. It is argued that the actions of women are, indeed always have been, crucial to the survival (or demise) of family farming and therefore to the process of rural restructuring. The problem lies in finding an adequate way to conceptualise the sets of social relations within families which give rise to particular outcomes. For example, why do families take particular courses of action and how are these structured by gender – specifically by the responses of farm women?

Early attempts to understand the evolution of family farming obscured the significance of women's influence by adopting a unitary concept of the farm family. More recent theoretical and empirical work has uncovered the deep gender divisions within farm families and the social relations by which women are subordinated. While such work has rightly criticised the 'naturalising' of gender roles within farm families it has sometimes given rise to a kind of patriarchal determinism by which women are rendered powerless, without influence. Underlying this is a concept of power relations as absolutist, as 'power over' rather than being inherent in the definition of action itself – the power to do or achieve or change something (Giddens, 1976). This chapter then is also about power and how we conceptualise it in farm families. In seeking to uncover farm women's influence, power relationships within farm families are seen as being two-way. Social reproduction involves what Giddens

(1979: 149) calls the dialectic of control whereby all power relations are reciprocal, however uneven the distribution of resources involved. Everyday life at the micro level of the family farm is a process of negotiation between women and men within the context of a wider set of macro forces which clearly subordinate women.

The empirical material in the chapter is drawn from a study of Irish farm families carried out between 1989 and 1991. This reveals how some Irish farm women have managed to achieve a significant lessening of their subordination through negotiation of power relations in everyday life. More fundamentally, through their role as mothers with responsibility for child-rearing and education, farm women's distinct influence over the future of the family farm through their control over social reproduction is uncovered.

Gender and family farming in capitalist societies

Attempts to understand the dynamics of family farming in capitalist societies have until recently paid very little attention to gender issues. Structuralist explanations of agrarian change in which family farming is viewed as a stage in a process of increased capitalist penetration into agriculture have not addressed the internal structure of the farm family at all, concentrating instead on the subsumption process. Others have argued the need for actor-oriented approaches (Long et al., 1986; Marsden, 1991), pointing out that purely structuralist explanations cannot capture the complexity of responses to capitalist expansion in agriculture. In this context the concept of survival strategies may seem to avoid the pitfalls of seeing farm families as hapless victims of the relentless forces of capitalism, yet it does imply a unitary idea of the farm family by not allowing for the existence of unequal relations or different interests within it (Redclift, 1986; Crow, 1989). Even when the idea of patriarchal control is incorporated into accounts of family farming based on the concept of survival strategies, it can be in a generalised deterministic way so that the 'naturalness' of gendered divisions of labour is replaced by the 'naturalness' of patriarchal control (see Pile, 1991). Focusing on survival strategies to account for differentiation in agrarian restructuring, does not allow us to capture what happens inside the family and whether the actions of men and women differentially affect outcomes (Redclift and Whatmore, 1991).

In Ireland, while few studies have put farm women at the centre of the analysis (but see O'Hara 1987, 1990; Duggan, 1987; Shortall, 1992), the farm family itself has received quite a lot of attention. This work was stimulated by Arensberg and Kimball's classic study of Irish farm families in the 1930s which, although functionalist in theoretical orientation, provided a detailed account of a highly segregated gender division of labour and family interaction on peasant farms in which women were clearly subordinate. Their work provided the starting point for a number of subsequent studies, most notably the work of Hannan and Katsiaouni (1977) who examined the task and decision-making involvement of farm husbands and wives (by interviewing both in great detail). Although failing to recognise gender as a social division within farm families,

Hannan and Katsiaouni did draw attention to inequalities within them, particularly the significance of husbands' power over the pattern of family interaction. They also put much emphasis on the quality of affectional relationships between spouses as an important influence on the division of tasks. In this sense their work foreshadowed later feminist concepts such as Whitehead's (1981) idea of the 'conjugal contract'. Their assertion that family roles are nowadays negotiated rather than culturally prescribed and that women frequently lose the marital battles over roles, resulting in a high degree of dissatisfaction among them, implies a degree of resistance and agency among farm women sometimes absent from more contemporary feminist studies.

Studies of family farming informed by feminist analysis are comparatively rare and recent. Central to feminist theorising is the concept of patriarchy as 'a system of social structures and practices in which men dominate, oppress and exploit women' (Walby, 1990: 20). Delphy and Leonard (1992) argue that capitalism and patriarchy are two distinct social systems which influence and structure each other and that the family is the locus of patriarchal exploitation. Women are exploited in the family, not because of the work that they do, but because of the relations of production in which they work (family-based households) and the fact that their work is unpaid. Even though farm wives produce so visibly for the market, they are just as subordinated as non-farm women because of the relations of production (i.e. the family) in which they live and work – they work unpaid for the Head of Household (HoH). Consumption within families is also unequal, with men and older male children being more privileged than women or daughters (1992: 146). Transmission of property and resources also favours men over women, specifically in farming where sons generally inherit the farm, but also because resources are distributed to individuals according to their status as persons, differentiated by age, sex and marital status.

Delphy and Leonard's work is unique and important in going beyond the labour and decision-making processes and examining transmission and consumption in order to reveal the gender-based structured inequalities within farm families. However, although they do show very clearly how transmission and consumption practices subordinate women and reinforce inequalities associated with the division of labour, it is the labour process itself that they identify as the principal site of women's subordination (1992: 18). This has the effect of creating a kind of reductionism by which women's influence (on social reproduction, on children, on ideology) cannot easily be accommodated. Also the concepts of HoH and paid/unpaid work do not seem robust enough to carry such a large theoretical edifice, especially in family farming where payment does not come in the form of an individualised wage. At the micro level of the farm, family social relations are complicated by the fact that production and consumption are not functionally separated.

Delphy and Leonard accept that they cannot pick up the responses of women to the constraints associated with their subordination. Although they stress that they do not wish to portray women as colluding in their own oppression, the weight of their arguments does appear to leave little room for agency so that women appear as 'victims, robots or fools' (Stacey, 1986). Such analyses cannot address women's resistance to subordination or the specificity of local conditions and cultures. Yet women's resistance can affect not only their own lives in specific circumstances but also social formations in the wider society. Berlan Darque has documented a variety of responses among French farm women who have negotiated quite different sets of relationships within the confines of the patriarchal farm family, and in the process gained considerable autonomy by constructing a different approach to professional work (1988: 228). Bouquet (1984) has also shown how the commercialisation of the domestic sphere – the taking in of visitors – ensures the reproduction of the farm household. Coleman and Elbert (1984) and Elbert (1988) have also highlighted the way in which farm women contest and cooperate at the same time, thus 'demonstrating form of feminism that reaches beyond any simple definition of autonomy or individualism' (Elbert, 1988: 263).

Whatmore's (1991) rigorous efforts to penetrate the black box of the family farm through a 'feminist reconstruction' of Marxist political economy is undoubtedly the most sophisticated attempt to incorporate gender relations into an analysis of family farming. Arguing that conventional political economy cannot accommodate a theory of the internal structure of the farm household, she has put forward a theory of *domestic political economy* which incorporates patriarchal gender relations into the commoditisation model. Patriarchal gender relations operate at the micro level of the family farm through the labour process, marriage and kinship ties, economic dependence, and ideologies of marriage. Whatmore shows how patriarchal gender relations intersect the commoditisation process through the organisation of family work and capital. The relationship between commoditisation, patriarchy and gender ideologies is not, however, as Whatmore admits, 'neatly synchronised'.

Whatmore clearly demonstrates the necessity of incorporating a theory of patriarchal gender relations into political economy theories about family farming and tells us much about the subordination of women on the farms she studied. While her theoretical position allows for the examination of other dimensions of power relations, she concentrates on the labour process and, because of this, farm women themselves emerge from her analysis as having relatively little room for manoeuvre. It is difficult to discern any significant actions by women which denote resistance to the patriarchal structures by which they are circumscribed or which can affect the evolution of the family enterprise. Although Whatmore does refer to the 'structural tensions' within the gender relations of the family farm as being potentially transformative (1991: 144), she sees the limited collective action of women as being the only evidence that they are taking action because they are dissatisfied with their lot. Within the farm family, they appear trapped by the twin burdens of patriarchy and commoditisation.

The analysis in this chapter seeks to build on and extend Whatmore's work. It is based on the conviction that, while the labour process is central to understanding gender relations in farm families, it is necessary to consider other aspects of the relationship between women's actions and the reproduction of family farming. These include their involvement in consumption and transmission, but particularly the significance of the mother (as opposed to wife) role and how this structures their actions.

Women on family farms in Ireland[4]

Relationships within the farm family in Ireland exist within a cultural heritage of gender ascribed roles and a wider gender order of agriculture in which women are subordinated. Nevertheless investigation of these relations at the micro level of the family farm reveals considerable variation in women's relationship to the family enterprise, as well as the nature of the conjugal contract and their own understanding of that relationship. Detailed interviews with sixty farm women in the east and west of Ireland revealed four distinct categories of women structured by their involvement in the family farm as an enterprise and their understanding of that involvement.

Working for the farmer

These women's working arrangements, involvement in decision-making, access to income and assets, and own sense of their situation are defined along patriarchal lines. There is an established pattern of control on the part of husbands, and such women often describe themselves (and their husbands) as old-fashioned. They have a strong consciousness of being constrained by patriarchal power relations. This is expressed as lack of 'independence', not having their own money, not having a say in decisions, being taken for granted and so on. Not all are equally explicit about this nor do all have a strongly contested conjugal relationship. There were 22 per cent (13/60) in this category.

Working for the family farm

These women's working arrangements, involvement in decision-making, control of assets and income, conjugal relationship and own evaluation of their lives indicate a significant improvement in their status, as we shall see below. Forty per cent (24/60) were in this category.

Farm homemakers

These women are quite detached from the farm as a family enterprise and are almost completely confined to the domestic sphere. In this sense they are little different from the wives of other self-employed workers. Fifteen per cent (9/60) were in this category.

Farm women in non-farm paid work

These women are involved in off-farm work which has differing consequences for their relationship to the family farm and the future of the enterprise itself. Twenty-three per cent (14/60) were in this category.

The women in each category experience their involvement in family farming in quite distinct ways and are to a greater or lesser degree constrained by the patriarchal structures of family farming. Those in the first category are subordinated by a hierarchy of conjugal roles by which they are identified as helpers in the farm enterprise and wives and mothers in the home. They typify the women that Delphy and Leonard describe as 'working unpaid for the head of household'. Those in the third category are quite detached from the farm as a family enterprise, so that their predicament can be understood as being similar to that of women married to waged, or other self-employed, workers who are full-time homemakers. In the next two sections I focus on the remaining two categories – women working for the family farm and farm women in non-farm paid work – in order to show in the first case, how within the confines of the farm family women can construct a social relationship involving a significant lessening of their subordination. In the second case farm women, by engaging in off-farm work, have managed to create their own sphere of influence and in some cases capitalise on the importance of their income for family farm continuity.

Working for the family farm – partners not victims

Farm women whom I have described as working for the family farm enterprise – as opposed to working for the farmer – perceive themselves as being in a partnership. They understand farming as a 'family enterprise' and have a strong sense of involvement in the farm as a business and in farming as an occupation. In practice they participate fully in all aspects of the farm operation in terms of management and decision-making, although there may be certain tasks that they do not undertake, but by choice rather than direction. They describe farm work as something which they enjoy and to which they bring certain skills. On farms with more labour-intensive systems such as dairying and market gardening, they are very conscious of their labour input and its significance for the enterprise, realising that they are indispensible, even if their work is not 'officially' visible. They speak also of the satisfaction of seeing animals thriving, crops growing, of sharing tasks and of being involved in a family project. They have a strong appreciation of the lifestyle of farming, of 'being your own boss', of being apart from the strictures of paid employment and of having control over their work, however arduous.

The family enterprise is described in terms of 'we' and 'ours', rather than the 'his' and 'theirs' typical of farm women more distant from the family enterprise. Likewise when discussing difficult times or tighter margins in agriculture they do so in terms of how the family as a group might respond or be affected. Those who have been through serious financial crises describe joint negotiations with financial institutions and women themselves often take on the role of financial manager. Indeed they are frequently more adept at handling financial crises than men, taking a more pragmatic approach when difficult decisions have to be made such as selling a part of the land. One of the women was negotiating the sale of a piece of land at the time of interview as the farm business was under severe financial pressure. She described her involvement in financial management – 'I do all the talking to the bank manager, my husband lacks confidence. He comes with me but he doesn't say anything. He is a good farmer but a bad manager.'

These women perceive earnings from produce sold on the market as family money, rather than an individual reward for effort, to which they have equal access and this appears to be borne out in practice as all of them have joint bank accounts. What they say about farm work and the money coming into the farm captures this:

> Money is thrown up on the shelf and we help ourselves to it until it is gone . . . I don't think of it as payment . . . Of course I'd like regular payment, who wouldn't, but not from the farm. It's not like that on a farm.

> I love being outside to tell you the truth . . . working with animals you see some success from your work and you have your own time . . . I think of the income from the farm as payment for the work that both of us do here.

> He [husband] doesn't handle any money at all. I get all the money and manage how it is spent. We have a joint bank account since we got married and everything else is in joint names. It's a what's mine is yours and what's yours is mine situation.

> I am the financial controller, I deal with the books, write cheques and see the bank manager and deal with the accountant.

The concept of a household 'head' in such cases is merely an imposed category, quite separate from what is actually happening in the working relationship. Furthermore, the payment for work cannot be attributed to a single individual when the income generated by the farm is handled in the way described above, particularly when there is no evidence that husbands appropriate part of the income for their own personal consumption before it has been made generally available.

The conventional sociological distinctions between productive and reproductive work would not be easily recognised by these farm women. The range of work that they do (both farm and domestic) is seen as being part of a way of life rather than work in the usual vocational sense. In common with farm women everywhere, they have primary responsibility for domestic work but they see farm work as a way of 'escaping' from household chores which are uniformly regarded as tedious and boring. Childcare is not viewed in the same light – as a set of tasks – perhaps because of the coincidence of location between home and work. One of the advantages of farming is that it allows women to combine childcare and other work and, for these women, having young children is not seen as an insurmountable obstacle to involvement in farm work. Change to a less labour-intensive enterprise, age or involvement in off-farm work are much more important influences on their farm task involvement.

Women who work for the family farm do not perceive themselves as subordinate in any way, but have created out of their involvement in farming a strong sense of identity with the family enterprise. They have a clear belief in the significance of their contribution to the family farm and a sense of solidarity with their husbands and other family members, who they perceive as having to work as hard as they do for no more personal gain. Although they experience the 'triple burden' of childcare, domestic work and farm work, they do not feel victimised by it. Rather they contrast the ease with which they can move between areas of work to the segmented lives of women in paid employment.

While they recognise that the work of farm women remains hidden and largely unnoticed, they understand this in terms of a set of macro patriarchal structures through which all women are subordinated. In their own sphere, this seems irrelevant. These women were quite unconcerned, for instance, as to whether they were registered joint-owners of the family farm, although most in fact were. Similarly, while they realise that men's virtual non-involvement in housework is neither desirable nor attributable to any 'natural' division of labour, they are realistic about the weight of culture and tradition and the role patterns established in men's own family of origin. At any rate, the women convey no sense of regarding the reproductive work in which they were involved as being of less value than farm work. This may have its origins in their experiences of their own mother's negotiation of the farm wife role. Many describe their mothers as being the most influential parent in their own household because they controlled the household income and were considerably younger (usually a consequence of a pattern of late farm inheritance in Irish farming) and better educated than their husbands.

It appears then as if these women have developed a particular way of contesting patriarchal structures by creating their own sphere of influence within the farm family. This is centred on their commitment to the family enterprise and is negotiated through a particular kind of conjugal or family contract, characterised by joint control and influence over the assets of the family enterprise. While the work regime is not necessarily characterised by egalitarian sharing of all *tasks,* the work *relationship* is such as to suggest a convincing lessening of the constraints associated with patriarchal power and achievement of considerable influence over consumption which is, after all, the ultimate objective of all production. On these farms there has been significant erosion of male authority so that the women have a considerable influence, not just on day-to-day production and consumption, but on the future of the family farm. This is signified by their involvement in decision-making and financial management. Such arrangements in everyday working life make divisions between productive and reproductive work, paid and unpaid work, meaningless to these women and of questionable value theoretically for understanding their situation.

Commitment to the family enterprise does not extend, however, to 'surviving at all costs'. Those on smallholdings are pragmatic about the future for family farming, and accept that the next generation will engage in farming only on a part-time basis. Even on the larger commercial holdings, where there will be a continuance of commercial farming into the next generation, most do not envisage a replication of the present family labour process, expecting that at least one half of the conjugal couple will be pluriactive. None sees their daughters as performing the same vocational role, except in the context of choosing farming as a desirable lifestyle.

Strengthening your hand – farm women in non-farm paid work

Retaining a pre-marriage occupation or returning to work after marriage is a recent and still relatively unusual pattern among Irish farm women. In 1990 an estimated 17 per cent of all farm wives had an off-farm job (National Survey, 1990). In the present study the proportion was somewhat higher at 23 per cent. With the exception of those who ran their own businesses all of these women were in white-collar jobs and more than two-thirds had been raised on farms. Apart from two women who had developed small businesses after marriage, all had retained their pre-marriage occupations throughout, rather than disengaging from, and then later returning to, paid work. They are a distinct and privileged category, not only in terms of the 'cultural capital' that they bring to the marriage but because their involvement in an occupation outside the farm changes not only the character of the family labour process but also the nature of the conjugal relationship. By generating an income of their own these women are in a much stronger position to challenge conjugal arrangements characterised by a pattern of male domination.

Working off the farm also changes their relationship to the family enterprise. For it is their occupational work, rather than the farm enterprise, which is central to their lives, both for the income it yields and the strongly felt occupational identity and sense of self-worth associated with it. Such women perceive themselves as being married to the farmer (as an occupational category) and not to the farm. As one young farm wife put it:

> There is now a new generation of farm women. Women married farmers in the past to be a farmer's wife. That doesn't happen any more. Most of the young women have jobs and work for money, although I'm sure most get job satisfaction too . . . I don't know what would make me give up work now. I can't think of anything that would, I'd hate to be at home all day.

For these women, generation of a personal income is a critical means of ensuring that they have secured what they consider to be a desirable standard of living. Indeed their marriage to a farmer is often premised on the expectation that it is their own earning power which will provide them with the material means to satisfy their aspirations:

> You have to have a certain standard in the house . . . It is not realistic to expect a living from a farm like this, and you just won't make money. I enjoy my job and we have a good quality of life, it is a good balance.

This was particularly the case in the western region where off-farm income is often crucial on smallholdings. Such women's contribution to the farm family income allows them a personal independence and higher material standard of living than their neighbours and protects the family from the risks associated with the uncertainty and unpredictability of farm income:

> It's very important to me to have my own money. I wouldn't like to be dependent at all. I spend the money on the housekeeping, the kids and myself and H. pays the bills like ESB [electricity] and the phone. I would hate to be asking for money, it's very demoralizing although some couples have a great understanding about this and just draw on what money they have. My own money is very important, our standard of living would be much lower if we didn't have it. It's a steady income, there every week, not like in farming.

> My income is nearly all that's available, even though it would probably be less than half of the income coming in. But we have a lot of commitments here.

> I couldn't live like that (if I had to ask for money). If I see something I want I have the cheque book. In other jobs the income is coming in every week so the husband will probably give a certain amount (to the wife), but in farming you could go for weeks and have nothing. The cheque for the cattle mightn't be as much as he thought and then what happens . . . in other jobs it is easier to budget.

In each of these farms the wife was a very significant contributor to the total family income, in some cases in excess of 50 per cent. The importance of their contribution to the family income strengthens their negotiating position in the conjugal relationship as regards their husband's participation in housework and childcare:

> H is willing to do housework and it is easy to do as much as me. When I am working he does more. It has to be like that, he takes over. I'm the main income earner here, I wouldn't be able to do it unless he was supportive.

None of these women had any significant involvement in the actual physical work on the farm and in some cases were quite detached from it, seeing it as an occupation like any other or as a nuisance – all work and no profit (in one case). Whereas on smaller holdings in the west, women's income was often crucial in allowing farm continuity, in the larger more commercial holdings in the east region the income was less materially important, except in cases where the farm was under financial pressure. In such cases women's capacity to generate an independent income takes on a new significance and women themselves experienced this as additional responsibility:

> My job accounts for most of the money coming into the house now, about 70 per cent. I couldn't stay at home. I have to go out and work . . . I feel pressure to work but I don't know if I could give up the wage packet either.

Even where there is critical financial pressure, women's incomes go to 'run the house' and/or pay the mortgage so that they have a much tighter control over the reproductive sphere than in cases where there is direct competition between farm and home. Each has her own bank account and a strong awareness of the financial autonomy and security associated with this:

> I would miss having my own money. I wouldn't like to give up my job. Not having your own money makes you completely dependent, and what if anything happens to your husband.

These women are also career oriented and speak of the fulfilment and satisfaction that they get from their occupation as well as the benefits of getting out of the house and interaction with work colleagues. They also appreciate the benefits of farming as a lifestyle and as a desirable environment for raising children.

Farm women in paid work therefore provide the farm family with a regular source of income which can be essential for the survival of the family enterprise. Such women use their financial independence to obtain in the first instance a higher material standard of living for the family and to retain considerable control over consumption. They also use this independence to negotiate a more egalitarian distribution of work roles, not always successfully. On larger commercial farms women's incomes were less significant to the maintenance of the family farming enterprise. Such women use their occupational status to detach themselves from the farming enterprise, relating to it as an occupational category rather than to a family business of which they perceive themselves to be part. As one young woman who was a nurse put it, 'it's the man, not the farm that you marry'.

Farm women as mothers: creating a different future

For many decades Irish women have demonstrated their feelings about the subordinate position of women on Irish farms by leaving rural areas and avoiding marriage to farmers, particularly on the smaller holdings in the west of Ireland (Kennedy, 1973; Brody, 1973; Breen et al., 1990). Their avoidance of marriage to farmers has been among the factors having a profound affect on rural social structure; by 1990 almost a third of all male farmers were unmarried. Education was an important avenue of escape for these women and higher levels of educational participation by farm daughters, compared to sons, has been interpreted as reflecting parents' wish to enhance their occupational and marriage prospects outside rural areas, where occupational opportunities are limited (Hannan, 1970; Conway and O'Hara, 1986). More recently Hannan and Commins (1992) have shown that farm children's educational achievements, even on the smallest holdings, have greatly surpassed those of the working class. In an environment in which educational credentials have become an important determinant of access to scarce employment opportunities, this represents a calculated effort on the part of farm families to secure desirable occupations for their children outside of farming.

Farm women are at the heart of this process. As Berlan Darque (1988) has noted for France, and the Irish data confirms, education is the farm woman's domain. All but one of the women studied are mothers and it is this aspect of 'reproduction' which gives the central meaning to their lives and their involvement in farming. The farm is a 'family enterprise' whose main purpose is the successful establishment of the next generation, whether on the farm or not. Only when children are successfully established occupationally, do parents contract their farm operation. In addition, on smaller holdings, mothers may take up off-farm work to finance their children's education. (Although none of the women in the present study had taken up off-farm work for this reason, some expressed a wish to do so and others pointed to neighbours or friends who had.)

Within the household farm women take almost complete responsibility for the education of children. This ranges from decisions about what schools children attend to supervision of homework and attendance at school meetings, as well as constantly reinforcing the value of a good education. Securing a good future for their children is at the centre of these women's 'reproductive' role and they identify this as a domain in which they have the major influence, both in realising the importance of education and in the actual practicalities of seeing that children study and avail of educational opportunities:

> I believe that education is very important, you could never put enough money into children's education. I kept them at their lessons, they didn't get away at night. There would be no discos during school times. We kept them at it although H. would be more lenient than me on this.

> I was the one that kept them at the books and drove them to school in T., 32 miles morning and evening because I thought it was a better school. And it worked, they will get their ambitions. Where there is a will there is a way. I kept them at the lessons with the back up of H. of course. I make the rules and they follow!!

> H. doesn't mind about education, it doesn't count. They can do what they like as far as he is concerned. Women are more education conscious, I don't know why. Men should know how important it is.

Farm women generally have a higher level of educational attainment than their husbands (reflecting the gender differences in attainment referred to above) and many attribute their predominance in this area to their greater appreciation of the value of education. However, it can also be interpreted as a strategy of resistance to the confines of farming as a career. Certainly, in the case of daughters, it represents an attempt to widen the opportunity set so that they achieve a degree of financial independence that they themselves are lacking. Mothers have adopted and shaped an ideology of autonomy for their daughters through ensuring that by having a 'career' they will never be financially dependent:

> It is a very good thing that women have their own careers and have their independence, I think that is very important. Otherwise there is a loss of education and brainpower . . . I would expect my daughter to keep on her career after marriage and children.

> I'd advise my daughter to keep on her job after marriage for the income and getting out and about and mixing with people. . . . It depends on the job too, if it is a routine job . . . but if you are a professional it is different.

> I'd say my daughters will work after they marry. M. says she won't get married. Don't marry a farmer I say to her, if you don't want to be mucking outside. Remember that about farming. We are really living on credit from the bank, it all has to go back (into the farm).

Daughters present during interviews confirmed these views, stressing the importance for women of having their own incomes and 'independence' – views, as noted above, articulated by women working off the farm, who are also of course important role models. The level of educational attainment achieved by daughters also bears out these aspirations and mothers express great pride in their daughters' achievements, particularly when they have been attained in traditionally male-dominated occupations.

Commitment to education for sons is less associated with resistance to gender roles than with resistance to farming as an occupation and the risks associated with farming. The families in this study were interviewed at a time when many were experiencing a drop in farm incomes. The future of farming was perceived by them as being very uncertain due to reform of the EC Common Agricultural Policy. Farming was also considered to be a very stressful occupation so that women regarded it as important that even potential inheritors (usually sons) have another occupational option. On smaller holdings selection of an heir was frequently postponed until one of the farm children had secured off-farm employment sufficiently close to the farm to make part-time farming feasible.

Farm women's control over children's education and associated occupational achievement represents an important way of resisting patriarchal power. This resistance has itself a gender dimension in that, in the case of daughters, it represents an attempt to ensure that the cycle of dependent farm wife is fractured and that the next generation have better choices. In the case of sons it represents disillusionment with farming itself or a recognition that pluriactivity is inevitable. What is important is that it is in their role as mothers, who can influence children's achievements through their control over social reproduction, that women's power is located. However powerless women might be in terms of control over property, labour or capital, children on farms are, as

Oakley says, 'the inalienable property of women' (1981: 228). Since children provide the next generation of family labour, this careful cultivation of withdrawal, or at least a shift in the terms of family negotiation, on the part of disillusioned women has important implications for the continuity of family farming as a social form.

Conclusions

I began this chapter by arguing that once we abandon a unitary concept of the farm family and accept the structured inequalities within it which subordinate women, we can then go on to investigate the implications for family farming and the wider social formation. From a feminist perspective family farming can be seen to be oppressive to women – their on-farm work is invisible and seen as unpaid, they often do not have ownership rights to the land, they are embedded in an industry which is publicly controlled by men. The issue of to what extent, and how, this patriarchal regime is extended to the private sphere of the farm family is of central interest to feminist analysis.

On family farms the gendered organisation of work and capital and the social relations within farm families are seen as being principal sites of patriarchal gender relations. The cumulative effect of much of the theorising and empirical work associated with the investigation of the patriarchal family farm has been to make farm women appear as victims, as being without power or influence. There is ample evidence from the Irish study of patriarchal gender relations at the micro level of the family farm. These are at their most extreme among the category I have designated as 'working for the farmer'. Yet the notion of Irish farm women as powerless collides with even casual empirical observation. Rather than investigate the social relations within families by which farm women are subordinated, the concern of this paper has been to focus on the ways in which they have managed to lessen the constraints upon them through becoming active partners in the farm enterprise or working off the farm, thereby greatly increasing their influence. More fundamentally, it has been shown that motherhood is a major source of influence for Irish farm women, even when they are strongly constrained by patriarchal family relations.

Women who work for the family farm know that their lives are circum-scribed by a wider gender order and cultural heritage by which women are subordinated and which makes the achievement of equality at best a long-term goal. Through their working relationships within the family enterprise they have fashioned their own form of equality and are conscious of their strength and influence. That this has happened through a negotiation of family relationships suggests that we need to bring the family much more to the fore in examining family enterprises and that patriarchal exploitation is not the same for every farm woman.

Women who work off the farm stand in a different relationship to the family enterprise depending on how significant their earned income is for its continuance. Farming cannot offer them the occupational identity which they achieve in off-farm work. On smaller holdings, or those under financial pressure, their income is crucial for the continuance of the enterprise. Their contribution to the farm is therefore indirect, mediated by the market and highly dependent on local labour-market conditions. The fact that it is so significant, however, strengthens the hand of these women in conjugal negotiation. On larger, more intensive enterprises women's off-farm work allows them a separate vocational identity and the farm as a *family* enterprise becomes less significant to them. As a patriarchal enterprise it can exist in parallel to their own vocational activities with little challenge from those women who wish to remain uninvolved. All of these women, of course, remain primarily responsible for household work and childrearing but there is nothing specific to the family enterprise which makes this predicament unique.

It is in their role as mothers that Irish farm women can perhaps exert the greatest influence on the future of family farming. Ironically, the very patriarchal structures which constrain them can also be seen as sources of their empowerment by constituting them in the category of wife/mother and assigning to them the crucial tasks of childrearing, socialisation and education – the placement of the next generation. In Ireland farmers' children have been exceptionally successful in utilising educational credentials as a means of upward social mobility (Whelan *et al.,* 1992) and farm women have been at the heart of this process of constructing the future for their children. This suggests that we need to pay a lot more attention to issues of power and influence within patriarchal structures such as family farming, moving towards a concept of power relations as reciprocal, even when they are clearly asymmetrical. Otherwise, we run the risk of overlooking farm women's influence and their responses to the constraints associated with patriarchal structures.

Few women, regardless of their own involvement in the family enterprise, foresee a future for their daughters in family farming. For those strongly constrained by patriarchal family relations, their insistence on creating the conditions whereby their daughters can secure occupations to guarantee them financial independence is a way of ensuring that their own circumstances are not replicated in the next generation. It represents a conscious strategy of orchestrating the withdrawal of women and future farm wives (in the event that daughters do decide to marry farmers) from active participation in the family enterprise. In so far as farm wives in the future are likely to retain their pre-marriage occupations and farmers to select wives who can provide the farm family with a regular source of off-farm income, this constitutes a fundamental shift in women's relationship to family farming. It has been precipitated by farm women's rejection of the patriarchal structures of family farming and reinforced by the need for farm families to insure against risk by securing regular off-farm income. It has been missed by much of the empirical research on farm women which focuses on the present generation,[5] and the theoretical work which ignores their role in social reproduction. It is not surprising in these circumstances that there is little evidence of political mobilisation among farm women. They have adopted a private rather than public form of resistance, which is nevertheless having a profound effect on the nature of farming as a family enterprise, the structure of agricultural production and, indeed, the wider patriarchal order.

Notes

1. Ireland, throughout this paper refers to the Republic of Ireland.
2. Article 45.2.v of the Irish Constitution reads: 'The State shall, in particular, direct its policy towards securing that there may be established on the land in economic security as many families as in the circumstances shall be practicable.'
3. In Ireland there is almost universal association between family and farm. Farm households rarely have members outside the family or kin group and the typical pattern is of a family grouping associated with the farm. Farm household and farm family are virtually synonymous.
4. The Irish material referred to here is drawn from a study of farm families in the east and west of Ireland carried out between 1989 and 1991. The study generated both quantitative and qualitative data which will be reported in detail in due course. Here I draw mainly on detailed personal interviews with sixty farm women which I carried out during 1991. The interviews covered a wide range of issues, the emphasis being on uncovering how women themselves make sense of their 'place' in family farming. The quotations in the text are taken from different women across a variety of farm situations. The letter H. denotes 'husband' throughout.
5. Gasson (1987) in a study of farmer's daughters in the south of England found that only 13 per cent of daughters in the study married farmers. The average farm size of these daughters' farm or origin (195 hectares) was well above the sample mean.

References

Arensberg, C.M. and Kimball, S.T. (1940) *Family and Community in Ireland.* Harvard, Harvard University Press, re-issued in 1967.

Berlan Darque, M. (1988) The division of labour and decision-making in farming couples: power and negotiation. *Sociologia Ruralis,* 28 (4): 271–92.

Bouquet, M. (1984) Women's work in rural south west England. In Long, N. (ed.) *Family and Work in Rural Societies.* London, Tavistock.

Breen, R., Hannan, D., Rottman, D. and Whelan, C. (1990) *Understanding Contemporary Ireland: State, Class and Development in the Republic of Ireland.* Dublin, Gill and Macmillan.

Brody, H. (1973) *Inishkillane: Change and Decline in the West of Ireland.* London, Allen Lane.

Coleman, G. and Elbert, S. (1984) Farming families: the farm needs everyone. In Schwarzweller, H.K. (ed.) *Research in Rural Sociology and Development: Focus on Agriculture, Vol. I.* Greenwich, JAI Press.

Conway, A.G. and O'Hara, P. (1986) Education of farm children. *The Economic and Social Review,* 17(4): 253–76.

Crow, G. (1989) The use and concept of 'strategy' in recent sociological literature. *Sociology,* 23(1): 1–24.

Delphy, C. and Leonard, D. (1992) *Familiar Exploitation: A New Analysis of Marriage in Contemporary Societies.* Cambridge, Polity Press.

Duggan, C. (1987) Farming women or farmers' wives? Women in the farming press. In Curtin, C., Jackson, P. and O'Connor, B. (eds) *Gender in Irish Society.* Galway, Galway University Press.

Elbert, S. (1988) Women and farming: changing structures, changing roles. In Haney, W.G. and Knowles, J.B. (eds) *Women and Farming: Changing Roles, Changing Structures.* Boulder, Westview Press.

Gass, R. (1987) Careers of farmer's daughters. *Farm Management,* 6(7): 309–17.

Giddens, A. (1976) *New Rules of Sociological Method.* London, Hutchinson.

Giddens, A. (1979) *Central Problems in Social Theory.* Berkeley, University of California Press.

Hannan, D.F. (1970) *Rural Exodus.* London, Geoffrey Chapman.

Hannan, D.F. and Commins, P. (1992) The significance of small-scale landholders in Ireland's socio-economic transformation. In Goldthorpe, J.H. and Whelan, C.T. (eds) *The Development of Industrial Society in Ireland.* Oxford, Oxford University Press.

Hannan, D.F. and Katsiaouni, L. (1977) *Traditional Families?* Dublin, Economic and Social Research Institute.

Kennedy, R. (1973) *The Irish: Emigration, Marriage and Fertility.* Berkeley, University of California Press.

Long, N., van der Ploeg, J.D., Curtin, C. and Box, L. (1986) *The Commoditisation Debate: Process, Strategy and Social Network.* Wageningen, Agricultural University, Working Paper, 17.

Marsden, T. (1991) Theoretical issues in the continuity of petty commodity production. In Whatmore, S., Lowe, P. and Marsden, T. (eds) *Rural Enterprise: Shifting Perspectives on Small-Scale Production.* London, David Fulton.

National Farm Survey (1990) Dublin, Teagasc, Rural Economy Research Centre.

Oakley, A. (1981) *Subject Women.* Oxford, Martin Robertson.

O'Hara, P. (1987) *Farm Women: Concerns and Values of an Undervalued Workforce.* UCD Women's Studies Forum, Working Paper no. 2. Dublin, University College Dublin.

O'Hara, P. (1990) Prospects for farm women. In *Women and the Completion of the Internal Market,* Proceedings of EC Seminar. Dublin, Department of Labour.

Pile, S. (1991). Securing the future: 'survival strategies' amongst Somerset dairy farmers. *Sociology,* 25(2): 255–74.

Redclift, M. (1986) Survival strategies in rural Europe: continuity and change. *Sociologia Ruralis,* 26(3/4): 218–27.

Redclift, N. and Whatmore, S. (1991) Household, consumption and livelihood: ideologies and issues in rural research. In Marsden, T., Lowe, P.

68

and Whatmore, S. (eds) *Rural Restructuring: Global Processes and their Responses*. London, David Fulton.

Shortall, S. (1992) Power analysis and farm wives: an empirical analysis of the power relationships affecting women on Irish farms. *Sociologia Ruralis*, 32(4): 431–51.

Stacey, J. (1986) Are feminists afraid to leave home? The challenge of conservative pro-family feminism. In Mitchell, J. and Oakley, A. (eds) *What is Feminism?* Oxford, Basil Blackwell.

Walby, S. (1990) *Theorizing Patriarchy*. Oxford, Basil Blackwell.

Whatmore, S. (1991) *Farming Women: Gender Work and Family Enterprise*. London, Macmillan.

Whelan, C.T., Breen, R. and Whelan, B. (1992) Industrialisation, class formation and social mobility in Ireland. In Goldthorpe, J.H. and Whelan, C.T. (eds) *The Development of Industrial Society in Ireland*. Oxford, Oxford University Press.

Whitehead, A. (1981) 'I'm hungry, mum': the politics of domestic budgeting. In Young, K., Wolkowitz, C. and McCullagh, R. (eds) *Of Marriage and the Market*. London, Routledge and Kegan Paul.

CHAPTER 4

Engendering the Farm Crisis: Women's Political Response in USA

Katherine Meyer and Linda M. Lobao

Introduction

Accounts of the 1980s' US farm crisis provide contrasting pictures of farmers' political response. On the one hand, the popular media give the impression of heightened activism through focus on dramatic events such as protests over farm foreclosures, standoffs between farmers and law officials, and the agitation of fringe organisations. Farm women were often visible at these events, their activist role underscored by the films of the era, *Country*, *The River* and *Places in the Heart* (Friedland, 1991). The dominance of media portrayals is reflected further in Hollywood farm wives' Jane Fonda, Sissy Spacek and Jessica Lange, testimony about farmers' hardships to Congress in 1985. Scholarly research tells a different story. It suggests that farmers were relatively inactive due to lack of financial resources and support from other community members and organisations (Heffernan and Heffernan, 1986; Rosenblatt, 1990). Moreover, women seemed no more active than men (Friedland, 1991).

To the extent that the popular media focused on unique events and exceptional women, it obscures how farm women as a whole were touched by the crisis. Beyond media portrayals, we know little about whether discontent filtered down into most women's lives and if this spurred political activism. With few exceptions, the topic of farm women's political response during this period has been almost entirely neglected by scholars (Friedland, 1991). Firstly, most research on the crisis focuses on financial impacts on the farm unit and on the farm operator, who, whether by self-designation or research design, is

69

70

almost always male. Secondly, although women's farm and household contributions are increasingly recognised, their political contributions remain less
explored. The consequences of contemporary farm restructuring for women, if
analysed at all, tend to be confined mainly to the division of farm labour and to
off-farm work. Women also tend to be viewed as generally passive reactors,
modifying their work roles in response to structural change, rather than as
actively shaping the sociopolitical environment.

Most studies of political attitudes and behaviour are directed towards
routine processes such as voting and office-holding. As noted by a number of
analysts, this misses much of the political activity of subordinate groups such
as women, ethnic minorities and the poor who have been marginalised
historically from formal channels of influence and/or who question the efficacy
of electoral politics (Jones, 1988; Morgen and Bookman, 1988). Rather, the
concept of political activism needs to be broadened to include women's
everyday efforts, evident in actions and discourse, to alter power arrangements
as well as their involvement in nonconventional activities such as protest
(Fraser, 1989).

In this chapter, we explore the gendered nature of the farm crisis and its
consequences for women's political beliefs and actions. Building from feminist
and political economy perspectives, we discuss how women may differentially
experience and interpret economic changes such as the farm crisis, which in
turn, shapes their distinct political response.[1] Our discussion is based on two
studies. We draw foremost from a survey of farm women and men conducted
in the Midwestern state of Ohio. Survey findings are supplemented with
personal interview observations from women leaders of farm organisations.[2]

Crisis and change in US farming

Crisis in the farm sector was manifest in the early 1980s as the monetarist
defeat of inflation, launched by the Reagan presidency, lowered land values
and as world-wide recession and a sharp rise in the value of the dollar reduced
the demand for farm exports. By 1986, about one-fifth of all farmers were
considered to be in financial stress and farm bankruptcies and foreclosures
were occurring at a rate several times that of the historical average (Leistritz
and Murdock, 1988). The crisis had an uneven effect across regions, farm units
and households. Midwestern farms were hardest hit, in part due to their
specialisation in cash grains which experienced declining markets for exports.
As is often noted, the crisis affected particularly middle- to upper-middle-size
commercial units that are less able to handle high debt loads and younger,
more highly leveraged farmers.

Changes in farming during the 1980s were not only the result of the
immediate financial crisis but also of long-term postwar trends. An increasingly
dualistic farm system had emerged, marked by relative changes such as the
increase in the number of small part-time farms, the decline of simple
commodity units or traditional family farms and the expanding market-share
of the largest farms (Goss *et al.,* 1980; Krause, 1987; Lobao, 1990).

Correspondingly, the class structure of the farm population became increasingly internally stratified away from the petty bourgeois ideal. Farmers' activism in previous epochs of economic crisis and change is documented in a rich literature. Over time, however, as agrarian class structure has become more differentiated, political interests have grown more divergent and less prone to the galvanising effects of crisis (Howe, 1986; Lobao and Thomas, 1992). This was particularly evident in the sociopolitical context of the 1980s. Firstly, this crisis did not affect all farmers equally. Larger, less highly leveraged operators stood to gain and often were the major purchasers of farmland from those who exited. Even farmers in roughly similar class locations experienced dissimilar effects as debt-load, commodity and period of entrance into farming varied. Farmers' interests were fragmented further by the organisations that have arisen out of differentiation, such as supply and marketing cooperatives and commodity associations. Of the traditional farm organisations the American Farm Bureau Federation is by far the largest taking a generally conservative, free-market stance towards farm policy and trade.

The uneven effects of the crisis, differentiated agricultural class structure and domination of conservative farm organisations would seem to mitigate against farmers' militancy during the crisis period. Moreover, this response parallels that found in studies of the general US population which point to depressed activism in the face of recent economic hardship and absence of mobilising organisations (Peterson, 1990). While individuals experiencing greater economic hardship may endorse more progressive political beliefs, their political activism is likely to be dampened due to lack of resources and a predominant 'individual ethos' that inhibits collective action (Peterson, 1990: 64).

The bases of women's political response

The 1980s' farm crisis thus occurred in a historical and organisational context that was not conducive to widespread militancy. Despite this generalised pattern, differences between farm women's and men's political stances and activism during the crisis period can be expected. The feminist literature delineates the ways in which such differences are likely to be manifested. Feminist perspectives ground gender differences in political response in women's structurally subordinate position and in their responsibility for reproduction (Morgen and Bookman, 1988; West and Blumberg, 1990). Socialisation and gender ideologies reinforce women's position. While these forces circumscribe women's lives, they are seen as subject continually to women's challenge, negotiation, and use as a base of resistance (Morgen and Bookman, 1988). As a consequence, Jonasdottir (1988: 42) asserts that:

> the background variable of gender is one of the most, sometimes *the* most differentiating factor in studies of political behaviour . . . Women to a greater *degree* than men, and in different *ways,* initiate, pursue, and support issues concerning bio-social production and reproduction, that is, those questions having to do with control over, responsibility for, and care of people and natural resources. (emphasis in the original)

Considerable theoretical debate over the precise origin and extent of such differences remains, however. Marxist-feminist perspectives particularly attribute women's stances as emanating firstly from their structural position in capitalist patriarchy. This confers lived experiences and the possibilities of consciousness development that set women apart from men (Eisenstein, 1981; Hartsock, 1983). Others, notably Gilligan (1982) argue from an essentialist standpoint that women's particular relationship to reproduction imparts commonalities that result in distinctly female ways of thinking and acting. More recently, feminists have questioned these conceptualisations and focused on differences *within* gender categories (Crosby, 1992). Race and ethnicity, age and generation, as well as class, make for disunity in women's structural positions and experiences. Differences between women and men over their stance on a variety of political issues have been documented. Women have been found to be more concerned with community welfare, more approving of state intervention in the economy, and less likely to support the use of force (Siim, 1988; Tilly and Gurin, 1990). However, researchers also point out that while women's and men's stances often vary, differences tend to be small and some have disappeared over time (Sears and Huddy, 1990). The modes by which women express their political interests are also seen to be distinct from those of men. Some have viewed women's structural position, responsibilities for reproduction, and gender ideologies as barriers to activism, particularly in routine politics. These include women's limited time and financial resources (Christy, 1987); the multiple claims for women's political attention (Mohai, 1992); and hostile organisational climates. Others have seen women's position and responsibilities as bases for activism. The 'solidarities of everyday life', in which women are linked to others in the community through shared status and work roles, provide a foundation for collective action (Tilly and Gurin, 1990). As with other subordinate groups, women's political activism is evident also in day-to-day personal resistance behaviours in the household, community and workplace.

The state also differentially affects women's lives and is particularly important to understanding women's political response in times of crisis. State action and control over cultural resources shape gender relationships and therefore may reinforce women's structural position. At the same time, programmes and policies enable women to defend their interests and secure autonomy from men. Feminist interpretations of the role of the state reflect these conflicting views. Marxist-feminist perspectives have often emphasised that the state oppresses women through its support of the patriarchal family and women's traditional roles and dependence on a male wage earner (see Morgen, 1990). This is evident in the two major ways in which state social provisioning takes place (Fraser, 1989). One set of programmes, such as social security and unemployment insurance, is contingent on participation in paid work and thereby on the male work record. The other, means-tested programmes such as welfare and food stamps, centres on the household. The former is a 'masculine subsystem' in which participants have rights. The latter is a 'feminine subsystem' in which participants are dependent clientele.

More recently, feminists have argued that the state has a paradoxical character (Morgen, 1990; West and Blumberg, 1990). The extent to which the state reproduces male dominance is contingent upon historical context and the specific issue. Piven (1985), for example, has viewed the welfare state as often advancing women's interests. Women's calls for state action in enhancing social welfare programmes have resulted generally in greater economic support and autonomy from men. Morgen (1990) argues that state policy may have unexpected outcomes. She provides two cases of state intervention into a women's organisation that lead initially to co-optation and later to progressive changes and new gender consciousness. From this perspective, the impact of state action on women's goals and collective action cannot be predetermined. Though the state treats women as lesser social citizens, at times, state action has been emancipatory.

Nearly all feminist understanding of women's response to changes in developed countries has come from outside family-based production. Workplace and household and the statuses within are separated, offering more independent bases for the politicisation of women's needs. Studies of women's political action in post-Fordism at least implicitly reflect this duality, with focus given to women's struggles at the point of production (strikes, plant closures) or at the point of consumption, such as tenant and welfare rights (West and Blumberg, 1990). Calls for state action imply invoking separate sets of programmes to deal with each arena of change. In contrast, enterprise and household intersect in the farm sector. Statuses in the household are transferred to the enterprise and changes in the enterprise are inextricably linked to outcomes at the household level. State intervention in the farm sector occurs nearly entirely on behalf of the enterprise (and therefore through the farm operator) rather than the household, as property ownership makes most farm families ineligible for public assistance. In this context, women's political response emerges in distinct ways that reflect the intersection of their statuses and experiences with regard to the enterprise, household and the state.

The gendered nature of the farm crisis and women's political response

Building from the feminist literature, the social bases of farm women's political response to the recent crisis can be outlined. As Whatmore (1991) points out, most women experience farming as 'farm wives', in structurally subordinate positions in the family enterprise. This position confers specific roles and responsibilities, subject to human agency, in farm production and household reproduction. It also situates women in critical junctures where economic change has occurred (Lobao and Meyer, 1991). That is, because the farm household is a unit of production and consumption situated in a particular community context, women particularly confront hardship and change in all three arenas. The ways in which women experience and interpret these changes is likely to structure their political response.

Most obviously, the recent crisis of the 1980s and longer term structural trends are changes in the sphere of production affecting farm households. Farm change is intertwined also with household well-being and adaptations, particularly the more a household is dependent upon farming for its livelihood.

The division of labour, off-farm employment decisions, as well as levels of family livelihood may be altered. Historically, family farmers have coped with low prices and other financial strains by cutting back on household consumption levels or 'self-exploiting' (Friedmann, 1978) and by seeking off-farm employment. While these strategies have enabled family farmers to survive in an agricultural system that has become increasingly concentrated and centralised over time, it has often come at costs of poor quality of life and high social-psychological stress. For households situated in farming-dependent communities, the crisis also had secondary and tertiary effects on the local economy. These, coupled with the broader restructuring of rural industry in the 1980s, meant that farm households might witness the deterioration of their communities.

All members of the farm household do not confront these changes equally, however. Women's position in production, reproduction, and as mediators between household and community, suggest that they would likely make more life adjustments. As Whatmore (1991) notes, women are situated in a 'patriarchal labour process' in which the timing, nature and outcomes of their work fall under men's control. Further, as studies of other populations have found, women's responsibilities for household consumption tend to sensitise them to changes in this arena to a greater degree than men (Tilly, 1981; Elder and Liker, 1982). Current work on farm women confirms their greater concern with consumption issues (Lobao and Meyer, 1991; Hsieh, 1993), feelings of hardship and higher levels of social-psychological stress relative to farm men (Walker and Walker, 1988; Duncan *et al.,* 1988). These outcomes have been attributed to women's multiple roles and to household consumption management.

During the farm crisis, women thus confronted the possibility of changes in farm production, household consumption and community. As the feminist literature shows, women have often called upon the state to address changes particularly in the latter two areas. Farm women would be expected to do likewise, though they are tied to the state in a distinct way. To the extent that state programmes and policies protect family farmers from the market, state actions may be seen as progressive, particularly in light of government free-market policies of the 1980s.[3] State intervention in the contemporary farm sector, however, is premised upon supporting the production exigencies of the enterprise rather than the farm household. A vast mix of policies and programmes provide state subsidised inputs, production controls and price supports. As noted previously, farm households are generally excluded from means-tested social welfare programmes due to their assets. Through support of the enterprise, the state reinforces traditional male production roles. At the same time, household survival and women's fortunes are tied to those of the enterprise and to the array of state programmes and policies that support it.

Most of our information about farm women and politics comes from studies of those who are active in farm organisations. Women broadly participated in turn-of-the-century protest movements such as the Populist Party and Farmers' Alliance (Fink, 1992; Wagner, 1988; Miller and Neth, 1988). However, Fink (1992) notes that they were largely in subordinate positions in these movements. Issues such as suffrage were not given serious or sustained concern and women activists rarely challenged the agrarian ideal of the male head of farm and household. According to Fink (1992: 24):

> Women were allowed to speak on established positions, but they did not challenge the political dictum that placed 'the man' at the centre of injustices toward farmers. The role of the woman, even in her political participation, was devoted to establishing the rightful supremacy of the (male) farmer.

Studies of the 1980s' crisis likewise centre on women who take activist stances in farm organisations (Hoff, 1992; Miller and Neth, 1988). As such, they may reflect more the experiences of the 'exceptional' rather than general woman. Common themes run through this literature, paralleling our earlier arguments. Women's activism tends to be built on their previous experiences in community networks. While economic hardship is generally seen as a barrier to participation for both women and men, women encounter special difficulties. Women members of a farm political action group studied by Hoff (1992) list 'household and farm work' and 'fatigue' along with 'money' and 'driving distance' as the major barriers to participation.

The gendered nature of the farm crisis becomes apparent in several ways which have implications for women's political response. First, women's objective experiences with regard to work roles and other life adjustments and their subjective interpretations tended to vary. In other words, women often experienced the farm crisis in different ways from men. Secondly, women's objective and subjective experiences would be expected to result in a differential political response. Greater experiences and perceptions of hardship tend to be related to more progressive political stances but not necessarily to political activism, at least of the conventional sort (Peterson, 1990). Finally, the farm crisis occurred in a socio-historical context in which men's experiences and exigencies have tended to override those of women. State programmes and policies and farm organisational platforms centre on the farm enterprise and *de facto* male operator rather than on the household and farm women. The historical institutionalisation of male interests and the contingent nature of household survival provide barriers to women's independent expression of needs and channel their political voice in particular directions.

Regional context and study samples

Out study is based on a survey of 497 farm women and 531 men in Ohio. Detailed description of the study and sampling procedures are described in Lobao and Meyer (1990). Ninety-eight per cent of the women and 90 per cent of the men are married, with the sample composed of 86 per cent matched couples. Thus, comparisons between men and women can be made which indirectly hold household and farm attributes constant. Median age is 51 for women and 54 for men. As is characteristic of the Ohio farm population, nearly all farmers are white. Farm and household characteristics typify the eastern Corn Belt pattern of smaller commercial family farms. Off-farm employment and a smaller farm size traditionally have provided farmers with partial insulation from debt and inadequate farm income. Even so, about one-third of larger, commercial operations had debt-to-asset ratios above 0.4, indicating serious to extreme difficulty.

Case-study material from a sample of approximately one hundred women officers in Midwestern farm organisations is used to supplement and clarify our survey findings. Four types of organisations were selected to give an even distribution of organisational type and stance on farm issues: general farm organisations such as the Farm Bureau and women's branches of these organisations; commodity groups; independent farm women's organisations such as WIFE (Women Involved in Farm Economics); and political action groups such as Prairiefire. Interviews were conducted in 1991 with leaders requested to recount their observations about farm women's responses to the changes of the 'crisis' period.

Changes in patterns of work, life experiences and perceptions

Women's roles in direct production activities followed those reported in earlier studies (Rosenfeld, 1985) and seemed little changed during the crisis. When asked to define their roles, about half the women selected 'farm homemaker', a person whose main farm activities involve running errands and traditional homemaking chores. About 14 per cent consider themselves full agricultural partners, sharing equal work and decision-making with their spouses. Only one woman considered herself an entirely independent producer.

Women were asked to report changes in work roles since the beginning of the crisis. Most reported that the time they spent at various farm tasks stayed the same. Over one-quarter, however, noted that their general involvement in farming activities had declined, with declines most notable in field work, taking care of animals and supervising hired labour. These changes may have reflected the downsizing of the operation over time or the effects of ageing, since men, too, tended to reduce the amount of work time in these areas. The greatest changes for women came in the amount of time they worked at an off-farm job. Twenty-eight per cent of women reported increases as compared to 17 per cent of men. About 44 per cent of women work off farm, working a median 35-hour week, typical of service-sector employment. A smaller proportion of men (33 per cent) worked off farm. Twelve per cent of women also reported informal employment, particularly childcare, crafts-making and sewing. Employment changes are not only attributable to the crisis as there has been a long-term trend of farm women's movement to off-farm employment.

Women were nearly wholly responsible for household tasks such as preparing meals and cleaning with 98 per cent reporting these as regular duties as compared to 6 per cent of men. A large gap between responsibility for childcare between men and women was similarly reported. Further, women were three times more likely than men to report increases in the amount of time they spent on household tasks from prior years.

The survey provides evidence of farm women's triple burden and greater role adjustments than their male counterparts. The case-study interviews of farm women leaders corroborated these findings. When asked about role changes, most made observations about farm women's movement into wage labour. At the same time, they noted that the inequities at home continued. A sixty-year-old woman officer in a general farm organisation stated: 'Some men helped with the child care, mostly the youngest ones. But they still resented doing women's work. They'll do as little as we allow them to get away with.' Another leader commended, 'The housework didn't get done if women left [for work]. If men left, women covered their farm work.' Such inequities were broadly acknowledged by leaders across our sample, irrespective of their age or political stance.

Ohio women's own perceptions and well-being in the face of the crisis were documented through the survey items. Women were significantly less satisfied with farm finances and life than were men.[4] For example, only 33 per cent of women as compared to 40 per cent of men would recommend farming as a career to their children or relatives. Women perceived greater economic hardship as indicated by questions referring to how often the household lacked food, clothing or medical care in the past year. About 11 per cent of women reported that they frequently had problems affording the kind of medical care their household should have and about one-fifth reported frequent difficulty in affording needed clothes. Relative to men, women had somewhat higher levels of social-psychological stress, and expressed greater feelings of time pressures and problems in balancing work roles. They also observed greater life pressures such as stress, depression, personal conflict, increased substance abuse and other forms of social instability among immediate family members.

Despite women's apparently greater stress and pressures, their tenacity in protecting farm and family from the crisis was a consistent topic mentioned by farm leaders. Typical comments included:

> Women always try to hold the farm together. They have to feed and care for the family while men keep the farm going. Family expenses are cut first. We [women] sacrifice our time and what we [personally] want to keep the family business together.

Another noted: 'I was mom and dad because my husband was concerned with the financial end. I tried to keep things as normal as possible for the family.' In sum, gender differences in experiences and perceptions were not large but tended to be consistent. Women bore differential costs in terms of their new and additional roles, increased stress and life pressures. Women more so than men seemed to experience the farm crisis not only as a crisis in production but also in family consumption levels and stability.[5] They observed deeper deterioration in family economic well-being and increased stress and behaviours destabilising to family life. They also recognised personal strains in their ability to meet family reproductive needs.

Political and organisational behaviour

In contrast to popular portrayals of the crisis period, there was little indication of militancy among either women or men. Only 2 per cent were active in farm political action groups such as the Family Farm Movement and Prairiefire. Two per cent took part in farm protests 'in the past few years'. Women and men were equally likely to participate in protest and farm political action groups. Women's independent farm organisations, such as WIFE, Women for Agriculture and American Agri-Women played a national political role in making Congress and the general public aware of the crisis. These groups are generally non-partisan and focus on the dissemination of information about agriculture. About 6 per cent of women were members of these groups. More frequently, however, women were members of women branches of general farm organisations, particularly Farm Bureau Women (20 per cent) and of commodity producers' associations (7 per cent).[6]

Our study of farm leaders indicates that farm women's organisational platforms, whether independent or branches, focused on production, trade and pricing issues. Concern for women's issues was limited mainly to rights as farm wives, such as inheritance and social security, rather than to broader feminist agendas. Even gender interests connected to consumption, such as household hardships, were relatively little addressed. Women's independent organisations and branches often offered educational and leadership programmes to upgrade human capital and provide better spokespeople for agriculture. A leader of a branch of a farm women's commodity group explained: 'We need to be cheerleaders for agriculture. That's women's role – a persistent cheerleader.' Women were seen also as having a certain 'superiority' over men in articulating political issues, as a fifty-five-year-old leader noted: 'The women were able to communicate better than the men. But then, women *usually do* communicate better than men.' The goal of women's participation seemed not unlike that described by Fink (1992) in the nineteenth-century farm movements. Farm issues and the male experience clearly came first.

A variety of other political and farm-related organisations claimed some women's attention. More than half of women were members of Farm Bureau and about 20 per cent belonged to farm-supply and marketing cooperatives. Eighteen per cent were members of work organisations such as teachers' unions. Two-thirds were members of church organisations. Forty per cent belonged to educational organisations such as the Parent-Teachers Association. Six per cent were members of (NOW) National Women's Organisation. Relative to men, however, women were less likely to be members of general farm organisations and to be less involved in most aspects of routine political behaviour, such as office-holding, attending public meetings and communicating with government officials. The exception was women's membership in church and educational organisations which exceeded that of men. These findings correspond to previous points that women participate less in formal politics but that community arenas are more frequent sites of women's activism.

Women's political stance

Although there was little evidence of militant political behaviour, tendencies towards activism could be seen in women's attitudes and feelings. They tended to take more progressive stances than men on a number of issues including the endorsement of state intervention in the farm and domestic economy, the need to protest and egalitarian gender attitudes. Women were significantly more supportive of government action to support family farming. More than two-thirds of the women thought that non-family corporate farms should pay higher taxes than family farms and three-quarters believed that the government should have a special policy to ensure that family farms survive. Support for state intervention in the farm economy also spilled over to progressive domestic initiatives. Women expressed greater approval of increased state spending for job creation, establishing national health insurance and making tax burdens more equitable across class lines. Women were more likely than men to approve of certain types of non-conventional activism such as protest. For example 53 per cent of the women but only 45 per cent of the men agreed that 'if farmers have a serious problem, they should organise to get what they want even if protests are needed'. The greatest differences in political attitudes concerned those related to gender. Women were more supportive of women in politics as indicated by their responses on questions tapping the legitimacy of women's political involvement and willingness to vote for a woman president. They expressed significantly greater approval of women working outside the home, the need for government-sponsored childcare and the need for husbands to participate in housework and childcare. Eighty-four per cent of the women and 71 per cent of men agreed with the latter need.

We have argued that women's position as farm wives situates them in critical junctures where economic changes are occurring. As a consequence, they experience work-load adjustments, life pressures and consumption hardships to a greater degree than men. That these experiences shape political stances and behaviour is supported through a correlation analysis from which we summarise the results.[7] In general, experiences and perceptions associated with women's structural position and responsibilities, were rather consistently related to progressive stances on the domestic economy, state support of family farming, and gender and women's roles. For example, women have less satisfaction with farming and experience greater economic hardship and role stress; as a consequence, they are more likely to advocate state intervention in farming and to support farmers' protest. These experiences spill over into progressive stances about the non-farm domestic economy as well. In addition to the effects of gender, we also found that class location and personal characteristics shape political attitudes as generally would be expected from other studies (e.g. Buttel et al., 1982). For example, women and men from smaller, part-time farms, employing little hired labour, with lower income and education tend to be more supportive of state economic intervention and farmers' protests.

In contrast, while farm women's experiences and perceptions as well as a more proletarian class location were related to progressive political stances, they were also related to lower political involvement in major farm organisations and conventional political behaviour. That is, those who were satisfied with financial conditions and farm life, who experienced less economic hardship, higher family income and education, and whose farms were larger and used more hired labour were more likely to be organisationally and politically involved. Moreover, there is evidence that the presence of young children and the need to work off-farm discouraged women's activism. In sum, our data indicate that larger, more affluent, male farmers were the major political players during the farm crisis period.

Farm women leaders' comments also bore out linkages between women's experiences and perceptions and their political response. Women's roles in bookkeeping and family budgeting made them recognise the seriousness of the crisis and women often 'saw the first inkling that things weren't panning out'. Some leaders noted that women were better able to connect hardships to the broader political economy: 'Women tried to make their husbands understand that it [the crisis] wasn't his own fault. It was bigger than that.' Some also mentioned barriers to women's political activism due to their multiple roles. A 52-year-old president of a farm women's organisation perceived a lack of men's involvement in housework and childcare during the crisis which 'added lots of stress on women who do everything – job, farm, and family work. This makes it difficult for women to be involved in agricultural organisations.'

Conclusions

Building on the feminist and other literature, we have argued that women's structural position as farm wives situates them in critical junctures where economic change occurs. As a consequence, their experiences and perceptions vary from those of men. During the 1980s' farm crisis, women were more likely to have assumed additional off-farm work while still continuing their near sole responsibility for household reproduction. Women were more likely to articulate the threats they face over consumption issues, to be dissatisfied with farm finances and life, and to experience more stress and life pressures. These experiences and perceptions tend to be related to more progressive attitudes both in the farm and non-farm sectors. Women believe more strongly that the state should redress socioeconomic inequity and are more favourable towards using non-conventional political means to do so. These same perceptions and experiences are related to lower involvement in conventional politics. Differences between men and women are not large, however, and it is clear that there is considerable 'disunity' within gender, not only by class but also with regard to personal life and socialising experiences (Sears and Huddy, 1990).

In contrast to popular portrayals we found little militancy among either women or men, with political involvement confined to conventional political outlets. There are several limitations of our study that suggest we may be underestimating farm people's activism. Our sample is confined to Ohio and has little variation in key political determinants such as ethnicity. In addition, because the study is based on existing operations, it is limited to those individuals whose financial conditions enabled them to survive well into the crisis period. There are also reasons why we might expect economic decline to have limited effect on farmers' activism. Characteristics of the farm population may be present barriers to organising them. These include their differential class position, uneven effects of the crisis and the tendency observed among US populations to react with depressed activism in the face of hardship.

However, our findings also suggest that militancy was discouraged by the dominance of affluent male capitalist farmers in the major organisational and political leadership roles and in setting farmers' generalised response to the crisis. It is possible that this segment of farmers and their organisations failed to define the situation as one of crisis and acted to diffuse, rather than mobilise discontent. Our interviews with women leaders suggest this possibility. When we told them we were conducting a study of the 'farm-crisis' period, several from conservative farm organisations responded, 'What crisis?' and preferred that we not use this term.

Further, even those organisations recognising the magnitude of the crisis tended to define it more in terms of the male experience. The crisis was viewed as centred in production and as jeopardising the job autonomy and self-worth of the male farmer. Neglected in platforms and programmes was the vantage of the farm women who coped with multiple roles, potentially low-paying rural employment, declining family consumption and yet who was expected to be, 'the glue that holds the household together' (as one leader commented). Farm women themselves did not directly challenge this public presentation of the male experience. The institutionalisation of male issues in the social structure of agriculture and the possibility for state policy interventions that occur mainly through the enterprise indicate that the farm crisis would be defined in production terms and its solution in state aid to the enterprise. The interconnection of the household and enterprise also meant that household consumption needs would be met, albeit indirectly, through enterprise support.

If the crisis had been defined in terms of women's experiences, associated more as we know with progressive farm and non-farm political beliefs, would outcomes have been different? Clearly, farm women would have still faced similar obstacles to political participation. However, had farm organisations focused more on women's perspectives, there would have been a greater possibility of linkage with progressive non-farm groups, such as the feminist movement, Jesse Jackson's Rainbow Coalition (which made some headway organising farmers during the crisis) and locally based community activist groups.

Focus on overt expressions of militancy and exceptional women does not capture the range of political responses to the farm crisis. It overlooks the changes that were occurring in the hearts and minds of women, their structural position and their potential for future activism. While the movement of women into off-farm employment adds new stressors, it provides a foothold of power in the household. Should women have responded during the crisis period, in contrast, through increased farm work, their labour and output would have fell more firmly under men's control.

There is also evidence of raised women's consciousness and incipient politicisation of needs. Women were more supportive of women in politics and of gender interests ranging from the need for national childcare to the role of husbands in housework. To what extent these stances stem from the crisis itself or broader on-going social changes is unclear. The leaders' study suggests that the crisis sharpened women's consciousness with regard to household inequities. Leaders of all ages and political stances expressed clear resentment with most men's failure to take on increased domestic duties in light of their wives' expanding commitments. In sum, during the crisis, a previously uncontested aspect of farm life, the household division of labour, became opened to public discourse and potentially further politicisation.

Farm women's differential beliefs and structural position indicate that they will be key to any future progressive struggles in the farm and rural sector. Firstly, women stand at the centre of mobilising a constituency at the point of consumption. In the transition to a post-Fordist economy, political mobilisation on the basis of production or purely class interests alone has become problematic. Mobilisation along other related bases, such as consumption needs and standards, has become increasingly important for fundamental social change. Women have been important political actors in consumption-related struggles over welfare rights, education and health care access, community development, and environmental quality. These observations, coupled with our findings on gender differences in political beliefs including support for protest, suggest that farm women, like their non-farm sisters, may be mobilised along a greater variety of consumption as well as production issues. Secondly, farm women, more so than men, seem better able to connect the experiences and perceptions arising from the various dimensions of their lives to one another and to broader social structural problems. Their experiences and perceptions in farming spill over into progressive attitudes about the non-farm economy as well as gender issues. Women's stances may thus provide the basis of future coalition building between progressive segments of the farm and non-farm sectors. Thirdly, as restructuring of the rural economy impacts areas unevenly, political struggle is more likely to be local and centred on community issues. Since the community is a traditional arena for women's political involvement, this is likely to nurture farm women's activism.

This picture of women during the US farm crisis has several implications for broader feminist research on women's political response to economic restructuring. Most broadly, it demonstrates that women's social structural positions and subjective experiences provide the bases of their differential response to economic change. Possibilities for mobilisation, political stances and modes of political action are grounded in the positions and experiences that set women apart from men.

Also, with gender, social formations differentially position women in relation to production, household and the state. In social formations such as family farming, where household and enterprise intersect, women confront overlapping structural barriers and ideologies that may operate to inhibit autonomous articulation of needs. Women's needs become inextricably connected to enterprise survival and to the gender relationships within. Women's relationship to the state also varies from that of other women, with claims coming mainly through the enterprise. As a consequence, women's political response to economic change will be limited and/or channelled in certain directions. For example, farm women's organisational platforms advocated state support of the enterprise but gave relatively little attention to women's independent interests which became articulated mainly through everyday discourse. Our study demonstrates that it is important to recognise that groups of women have different sets of relationships from the state and economy. Calls for state intervention have thus different meanings and consequences for women's status (see also Morgen, 1990).

Finally, what appears initially as the subordination of women's political interests may, in fact, be a more complex outcome. Farm women's focus on support of the enterprise can be seen to reflect short-term gender interests of household survival. Oppositional discourses emerged during the crisis, signalling the possibility for further politicisation of women's issues. Farm women's more progressive stances also allow for coalition building with non-farm groups which, in turn, has the capacity to transform production agriculture, including gender roles. Thus, even in times of apparent quiescence over feminist agendas, there may exist the spiralling of debate and the positioning of women's issues for newer rounds of political conflict.

Notes

1. Obviously, farm women are not a homogeneous group but differ by ethnicity, class, and other structural and personal attributes. Women are also involved in varying gender relationships within the household and community. For recent descriptions of these latter relationships, see Barlett (1993), Salamon (1992) and Whatmore (1991).
2. This research reports on projects supported by grants from the following institutions: the National Science Foundation under Grant SES – 8809467; the Ohio State Seed Grant Program; and the Ohio Agricultural Research and Development Center. This chapter is a contribution to regional research projects, S – 246, 'The Transformation of Agriculture: Resources, Technologies, and Policies', and NC – 184, 'Policy Implications for Farm Household and Rural Community Response to Economic Changes'.
3. Recent farm activist organisations and other new social movement groups often refer to themselves as 'progressive' rather than 'liberal'. They put forth platforms aimed at creating a more egalitarian distribution of social and economic resources and at regulating destabilising market forces.
4. Significant differences between women and men are reported based on t-tests.
5. Other significant gender differences in community perceptions and social networks that might be expected were not found. For example, farm women and men tended to be similarly satisfied with their communities and to have a similar number of social support networks.
6. Compared with Rosenfeld's (1985) national study, more than twice as many Ohio women were members of women's farm organisations and women's branches of general farm organisations. However, this likely reflects more regional than temporal differences as organisational membership of all types was higher for the Ohio sample.

7. The correlates of men's and women's political attitudes were estimated through zero-order correlations of the entire sample (women and men) and separately by gender. The same relationships tend to emerge whether one considers the entire sample or within gender. For example, men who are more like women in that they perceive greater economic hardship tend to have more progressive political attitudes.

References

Barlett, P.F. (1993) *American Dreams, Rural Realities: Family Farms in Crisis.* Chapel Hill, NC, The University of North Carolina Press.

Buttel, F.H., Larson, O.W., Harris, C.K. and Powers, S. (1982) Social class and agrarian political ideology: a note on determinants of political attitudes among full- and part-time farmers. *Social Forces,* 61(1): 277–83.

Christy, C.A. (1987) *Sex Differences in Political Participation: Processes of Change in Fourteen Nations.* New York, Praeger.

Crosby, C. (1992) Dealing with differences: 130–43. In Butler, J., Scott, J.W. (eds) *Feminists Theorize the Political.* New York, Routledge.

Duncan, S.F., Volk, R.J. and Lewis, R.A. (1988) The influence of financial stressors upon husbands' and wives' well-being and family life satisfaction: 32–9. In Martoz-Baden, R., Hennon, C.B. and Brubaker, T.H. (eds) *Families in Rural America: Stress, Adaptation and Revitalisation.* St. Paul, MN, National Council on Family Relations.

Elder, G.H., Jr and Liker, J.K. (1982) Hard times in women's lives: historical influences across 40 years. *American Journal of Sociology,* 88: 241–69.

Eisenstein, Z. (1981) *The Radical Future of Liberal Feminism.* New York, Longman.

Fink, D. (1992) *Agrarian Women: Wives and Mothers in Rural Nebraska, 1840–1940.* Chapel Hill, NC, The University of North Carolina Press.

Fraser, N. (1989) *Unruly Practices: Power, Discourse, and Gender in Contemporary Social Science Theory.* Minneapolis, MN, University of Minnesota Press.

Friedland, W.H. (1991) Women and agriculture in the United States: a state of the art assessment: 315–38. In Friedland, W.H., Busch, L., Buttel, F. and Rudy, A.P. (eds) *Towards a New Political Economy of Agriculture.* Boulder, CO, Westview Press.

Friedmann, H. (1978) World market, state, and family farm: social bases of household production in an era of wage labour. *Comparative Studies in Society and History,* 20: 545–86.

Gilligan, C. (1982) *In a Different Voice: Psychological Theory and Women's Development.* Cambridge, Harvard University Press.

Goss, K., Rodefeld, R. and Buttel, F. (1980) The political economy of class structure in US agriculture: 83–132. In Buttel, F. and Newby, H. (eds) *The Rural Sociology of Advanced Societies.* Montclair, NJ, Allandheld Osmun.

Hartsock, N.C.M. (1983) *Money, Sex and Power.* New York, Longman.

Heffernan, W.D. and Heffernan, J.B. (1986) The farm crisis and the rural community: 273–80. In Jahr, D., Johnson, J.W. and Wimberley, R.C. (eds) *New Dimensions in Rural Policy: Building Upon Our Heritage, Studies Prepared for the Use of the Subcommittee on Agriculture and Transportation of the Joint Economic Committee of the United States.* Washington, DC, US Government Printing Office.

Hoff, M. (1992) Women's perspective on the rural crisis and priorities for rural development. *Affilia,* 7(4): 65–81.

Howe, C. (1986) Farmers' movements and the changing structure of agriculture: 104–49. In Havens, A.E. with Hooks, G., Mooney, P.H. and Pfeffer, M.J. (eds) *Studies in the Transformation of US Agriculture.* Boulder, CO, Westview Press.

Hsieh, H. (1993) *The Bonds That Tie and/or Divide: State, Family and the Midwestern Farm Politics of the Late 1980s.* Columbus, Ohio, unpublished Ph.D. dissertation, Ohio State University, Department of Sociology.

Jonasdottir, A.G. (1988) On the concept of interest, women's interests, and the limitations of interest theory: 33–65. In Jones, K. and Jonasdottir, A.G. (eds) *The Political Interests of Gender: Developing Theory and Research with a Feminist Face.* London, Sage Publications.

Jones, K.B. (1988) Towards the revision of politics: 11–32. In Jones, K. and Jonasdottir, A.G. (eds) *The Political Interests of Gender: Developing Theory and Research with a Feminist Face.* London, Sage Publications.

Krause, K. (1987) *Corporate Farming, 1969–1982,* Agricultural Economic Report Number 578. Washington, DC: USDA, Economic Research Service.

Leistritz, F.L. and Murdock, S.H. (1988) The implications of the current farm crisis for rural America: 13–28. In Murdock, S.H. and Leistritz, F.L. (eds) *The Farm Financial Crisis: Socioeconomic Dimensions and Implications for Producers and Rural Areas.* Boulder, CO, Westview Press.

Lobao, L.M. (1990) *Locality and Inequality: Farm and Industry Structure and Socioeconomic Conditions.* Albany, NY, The State University of New York Press.

Lobao, L.M. and Meyer, K. (1991) Farm restructuring adaptations in household consumption, and stress among farm men and women: 191–209. In Schwarzweller, H.K. and Clay, D (eds) *Research in Rural Sociology and Development: A Research Annual,* Volume 5. Greenwich, Conn., JAI Press.

Lobao, L.M. and Thomas, P. (1992) Political beliefs in an era of economic decline: farmers' attitudes toward state economic intervention, trade, and food security. *Rural Sociology,* 57(4): 453–75.

Miller, L.C. and Neth, M. (1988) Farm women in the political arena: 357–80. In Haney, W.G. and Knowles, J.B. (eds) *Women and Farming: Changing Roles, Changing Structures.* Boulder, CO, Westview Press.

Mohai, P. (1992) Men, women, and the environment: an examination of the gender gap in environmental concern and activism. *Society and Natural Resources,* 5: 1–19.

Morgen, S. (1990) Two faces of the state: women, social control and empowerment. In Ginsburg, F. and Tsing, A.L. (eds) *Uncertain Terms: Negotiating Gender in American Culture*: 169–82. Boston, Beacon Press.

Morgen, S. and Bookman, A. (1988) Rethinking women and politics: an introductory essay: 3–29. In Bookman, A. and Morgan, S. (eds) *Women and the Politics of Empowerment.* Philadelphia, Temple University Press.

Peterson, S.A. (1990) *Political Behaviour: Patterns in Everyday Life.* Newbury Park, CA, Sage Publications.

Piven, F.F. (1985) Women and the state: ideology, power, and the welfare state: 265–87. In Rossi, A. (ed.) *Gender and the Life Course.* New York, Aldine.

Rosenblatt, P.C. (1990) *Farming is in Our Blood: Farm Families in Economic Crisis.* Ames, Iowa, Iowa State University Press.

Rosenfeld, R.A. (1985) *Farm Women: Work, Farm, and Family in the United States.* Chapel Hill, NC, The University of North Carolina Press.

Salamon, S. (1992) *Prairie Patrimony: Family, Farming and Community in the Midwest.* Chapel Hill, University of North Carolina Press.

Sears, D.O. and Huddy, L. (1990) On the origins of political disunity among women: 249–77. In Tilly, L.A. and Gurin, P. (eds) *Women, Politics and Change.* New York, Russell Sage Foundation.

Siim, B. (1988) Toward a feminist rethinking of the welfare state: 160–86. In Jones, K.B. and Jonasdottir, A.G. (eds) *The Political Interests of Gender.* London, Sage Publications.

Tilly, L.A. (1981) Paths of proletarianization: organisation of production, sexual division of labour, and women's collective action. *Signs,* 7 (Winter): 400–17.

Tilly, L.A. and Gurin, P. (1990) Women, politics and change: 3–31. In Tilly, L.A. and Gurin, P. (eds) *Women, Politics and Change.* New York, Russell Sage Foundation.

Wagner, M.J. (1988) 'Helping papa and mamma sing the people's songs': children in the Populist Party: 319–37. In Haney, W.G. and Knowles, J.B. (eds) *Women and Farming: Changing Roles, Changing Structures.* Boulder, CO, Westview Press.

Walker, L.S. and Walker, J.L. (1988) Stressors and symptoms predictive of distress in farmers. *Family Relations,* 36(4): 374–8.

West, G. and Blumberg, R.L. (1990) Reconstructing social protest from a feminist perspective: 3–40. In West, G. and Blumberg, R.L. (eds) *Women and Social Protest.* New York, Oxford University Press.

Whatmore, S. (1991) *Farming Women: Gender, Work, and Family Enterprise.* Basingstoke, Macmillan.

CHAPTER 5

Rural Women's Status in Family and Property Law: Lessons from Norway

Marit S. Haugen

Introduction

Gender equality, understood as equal rights for women and men, is a prominent goal in Norwegian society (Law of Equal Rights, 1978). An amendment to the act regulating the succession to farms was passed in 1974 giving women equal rights to inherit farms for the first time in Norwegian history. The right of succession is now determined according to age alone and not according to sex and age as was previously the case; thus we have formally established equal rights for both sexes. As a result, it might be anticipated that within a few years, half of all Norwegian intergenerational transfers of farms would be to women. Recent studies show, however, that young women are less likely than young men to take over their parents' farm and that they seem to waive their inheritance in favour of their younger brothers (Johnsen, 1986). The central theme of this chapter is to consider how best to explain the discrepancy between the legal rights and the practical status of women as successors of farms.

Rural inheritance, the transfer of property down the generations through time, has received some attention from rural sociologists (Gasson *et al.,* 1988; Symes, 1990; Potter and Lobley, 1992).[1] Their main focus has been on kinship relations and the viability of family farms. The question of recruitment to the farm is central for most farmers. The thought of turning over the farm property to the next generation in better condition that it was when they took it over themselves is the most important motivating factor for building up the farm. If none of the children is willing to take over the farm, much of the work invested has been for nothing.

Less attention has been placed on gender issues connected with inheritance. Bouquet and de Haan state the obvious, but often undervalued, fact that the unequal distribution of rights in property within the family can result in differential attachment to the farm or even conflict:

> The transfer of property from one generation to the next touches upon processes of exclusion and inclusion among members of the domestic group, as rights in property are constantly negotiated and distributed according to culturally accepted rules of authority, equality, solidarity and residence. (1987: 248)

To choose to exercise one's allodial right is not only a decision about a career and a place to live, but also a choice of lifestyle, environment and continuing the family tradition and history. Sometimes the choice involves tensions within the family because of conflicting interests either between parents and heir, or between siblings. The conflict is not so much a question of juridical right, as a moral dilemma for the family members involved.

Although women's formal rights to inherit farmland vary, in Western countries it seems to be a common belief that a son is a potential farmer while a daughter will either marry a farmer or marry a non-farmer and leave agriculture (Salamon and Davis-Brown, 1988). Implicit is a sex-typing[2] of work and status; a farmer's occupation is a *man's* job. Hirschon (1984) argues that more systematic attention should be directed to the property factor in the analysis of women's position because access to, and control over, property is one crucial indicator of the power balance between women and men.[3] She states 'Women seldom contest for land to which they might be legally entitled and tacitly waive their inheritance in favour to male kin' (p. 17).

The persistence of patrilineal inheritance transmits the belief that it is men who have the legitimate right to the land, while women as wives and daughters are continuously disinherited (Shortall, 1992: 444). In the UK Gasson *et al.,* (1988) argue that the gross inequalities in gender relations in agriculture are rooted in customary practices concerning the transfer of property rights in family-owned farms, rather than in statutory law. Moreover, there is no necessary connection between ownership and recognised occupational status. Whatmore (1991) found in her study of family farms in Britain that male partners were seen as the 'farmers' even when the woman owned, or part-owned, the farm. Salamon and Keim (1979) suggested that in the United States women who actually owned land, allowed men to exercise control over the land.

Historical background: the case of the law

The Norwegian law regulating succession to farms goes back to 1821 (founded on a law from 1274). The main argument for keeping the law intact was to secure the transmission of land within farm families, preventing land from becoming a commodity and an object of capital speculation. Further, farmers, through tradition and socialisation, are regarded as the best cultivators of the land. To prevent division of farm land into small parcels and to secure the viability of the farm, only one of the heirs, normally the eldest son, could take over the farm; buying out his sisters and brothers. However, the law of succession to farms came into conflict with the ideology of gender equality and social justice which has informed Norwegian political institutions in the twentieth century. In the early 1970s the act was changed so that daughters and sons would have the same right to take over the (family) farm.

The amendment was a result of an on-going struggle for equal rights in the rest of society and not of a desire for equality specific to agriculture. In fact, the change in the law challenged the preconception that only men could be farmers and heads of family farms. The farmers' organisations themselves were especially sceptical about discontinuing the tradition of the farm going from father to son, and about the consequences of such a change. Many feared that the survival of the family farm would be threatened if the daughter married a man not interested in farming. The debate illustrated the lack of confidence in women's ability to farm themselves. Women as farmers were a token and invisible minority who were never held up as an example that women were already in a farmer's position.

The social changes that are now taking place have been characterised as a movement away from a society where the segregation of sexes and male dominance were legitimate expressions of a social order, to a society where integration of the sexes in all areas of society is the expressed ideal. However, female subordination still prevails, although more subtle and hidden than before (Haavind, 1992: 49). Here, we are concerned with the period of upheaval between the old patriarchal ideology in agriculture and the new ideology of equality where women and men have, in principle, the same rights and obligations. The analysis centres on the inadequacy of juridical equality in a context of social inequality. I will use a sample of young girls and boys with rights of succession to a farm to illustrate how their 'gendered' experiences influence their possibilities and choices.

Research has shown that girls are less likely to exercise their right to take over a farm than boys (Johnsen, 1986; Ølnes, 1989). Johnsen (1986) found that while seven out of ten boys say that they are planning to take over, only three out of ten girls say the same. Johnsen concludes that the younger brother appears to be the most important reason for many of the girls' planning not to take over the farm. Further, girls postpone making the choice longer than the boys; the consequence of this may be that they unconsciously make a decision not to take over the farm by the other choices they make in the meantime, for example education, career and choice of partner (Ølnes, 1989). I pose questions about how the differences between girls' and boys' future plans regarding the farm can be explained. I will analyse their upbringing and the influence of their parents. I also look at the attitudes of parents towards girls and boys, both expressed attitudes and the actual behaviour. These girls and boys have grown up in Norwegian society of the 1970s and the 1980s, which was constantly marked by the debate on women's rights and efforts towards greater equality. To what extent are their thoughts and actions influenced by the ideal of equality? Does this come in conflict with the expectations they meet with on the part of others?

Theoretical background

In virtually every society women and men conventionally perform different types of work. Some tasks and occupations are defined as 'men's' and others as 'women's'. Sex-typing of work may vary according to time and place (Bradley, 1989). There is a tendency for technological innovations to lead to a polarisation between 'women's' jobs and 'men's' jobs (Hacker, 1979). As Norwegian agricultural work has become more 'scientised', the work has become masculinised (Almaas *et al.,* 1983). Although women have always made a significant contribution to the day-to-day running of the family operation, the position as *farmer* is traditionally considered a 'male' position.

Farm children, like other children, are born into a gendered world. Parents raise their children to become girls and boys. Already from birth, children are treated differently, whether consciously or unconsciously. We give girls other attributes than boys; we encourage suitable behaviour through recognition and reward and we set up negative sanctions for unacceptable behaviour. In this way, girls and boys learn what is expected of them; they learn a gendered behaviour (Bjerrum Nielsen and Rudberg, 1989). Gender becomes incorporated into individual identity, tying a person's consciousness about him/herself to a specific gender identity (Harding, 1986). West and Zimmerman (1991) explain how this 'gendering' is incorporated by individuals themselves and in this way understood as something normal and natural:

> New members of society come to be involved in a *self-regulating process* as they begin to monitor their own and others' conduct with regard to gender implications. The recruitment process involves not only the appropriation of gender ideals but also *gender identities* that are important to individuals and that they strive to maintain. Thus gender differences, or the sociocultural shaping of 'essential female and male natures', achieve the status of objective facts. They are rendered as normal, natural features of persons and provide the tacit rationale for differing fates of women and men within the social order. (p. 29)

It is essential that the farm family succeeds in socialising one of the children into the lifestyle to ensure that the farm will continue in the family (Potter and Lobley, 1992). Parents' role in the socialisation process is central and even more so on farms where work is closely intertwined with family life. As the main goal for most farm families is to secure the succession of the farm, and this has historically been secured through patriarchal inheritance, the principle of gender equality is likely to be considered less important.

Even as women and men become more alike, women move out into the working world and the overlap between the life of a woman and the life of a man increases, it appears that they still articulate different systems of common sense and rationality, created socially by different experiences. The explanation of women's and men's different 'rationality' is tied to the division of work between the sexes. This gender division of labour gives women other experiences than men and socialises them in different ways. Prokop (1981) explains that women and men have different value orientations because women are socialised to be responsible for the caring functions within society. Thus, they develop a need-oriented communication that is useful in close personal relationships. Sørensen (1982) talks about a female *rationality of responsibility* as opposed to a male *technical-economical rationality*: while women are driven by the consideration of others, men are driven by the reasoning that efficiency in attaining a given goal is primary. The term 'rationality of responsibility' implies a conception of women as rational actors who choose to take responsibility for others. Gilligan (1982) has argued that women's approach to morality is different from men's. Women's morality, she argues is situationally and contextually based ('the ethic of care') and they are much less likely than men to fall back upon moral rules of a generalisable and abstract kind ('the ethic of right'). Women and girls will try to resolve a moral dilemma in which there are conflicting claims or considerations in such a way that no one gets hurt, if necessary themselves making a sacrifice rather than expecting it on the part of others. Women have been described as 'the flexible gender'.[4] Men and boys, by contrast will tend to respond by developing a set of rules which will secure a just or fair outcome, and this will often entail prioritising claims. As men's rationality is given priority and a higher value in our society, the result is a subordination of women's interests.

Women's rationality of responsibility and orientation towards others can work in two directions when it comes to deciding whether or not to take over the farm. The final decision may be in conflict with the girls' individual interests and wishes. Looking at the use of the legal right to a farm as a 'moral' question it should mean that girls more than boys waive their right if it comes in conflict with the interests of others. On the other hand it also means that girls, more than boys, might feel obliged to take over the farm if none of the siblings wants the farm.

To explore these 'moral' questions in practice, I present an analysis based on in-depth interviews with 19 girls and 15 boys, all with rights to the succession of their family farms, in four municipalities. Young people aged 16 to 20 were chosen for the study because they are in a phase of life where they have to consider the future, and make significant decisions considering education and careers. A criteria for being included in the study was that the heir had younger siblings.[5] Heirs were interviewed on their own, at home, during 1987 and 1988. Interviews usually lasted between one and two hours. A total of 31 fathers and 29 mothers were also interviewed in order to get a more thorough picture of the individuals' family situations.

Being a farmer – too heavy work for a woman?

Agricultural work is, in some aspects, physically demanding work, although mechanisation has reduced these demands tremendously. Now there is greater need for managerial and technological skills to operate the farm. Common myths of natural endowment and female incapacity have been disproved by women who successfully run farms by themselves and who operate the farm machinery (Haugen, 1990a). However, myths about strength and skills regenerate themselves even in the face of quite recent evidence as to the

Table 5.1 Are you planning to exercise your allodial right?

	Girls	Boys
Yes	1	8
Yes, probably	4	3
Haven't decided	8	1
No, probably not	2	3
No	4	–
N	19	15

competence and capability of women in farming (Bradley, 1989). We might expect such myths to inform the arguments used by girls themselves for not using their allodial rights. Table 5.1 shows how girls and boys plan to use their allodial rights.

In line with Johnsen's study (1986), most of the girls do not know if they are going to use their allodial right, while most of the boys have decided to take over the farm; and more girls postpone their final decision for longer than do boys. The traditional argument, that farm work is too physically hard for women, was mentioned by none of the girls as a major reason for not using her allodial right. Their reasons for being unlikely to use their allodial rights fall into two main categories; relational reasons (younger brother with more interest, parents prefer younger brother, choice of a partner); or reasons connected to working conditions (too tied down, little free time, low income). Three of the boys said that they were (probably) not going to take over the farm. All of them said that they were not interested in farming. Typically they all came from quite small farms, considered to be farms without a future. Among the girls there was no connection between farm size and the decision not to take over the farm.

The majority of the parents (68 per cent, N = 59) agreed with the statement that 'The occupation of farmers requires physical strength.' This did not necessarily mean that they believed that *women* in general do not have the necessary strength, but 57 per cent (N = 58) of parents believed that it is more difficult for a woman than for a man to operate a farm. As shown in Table 5.2, it is common for parents to be of the opinion that women and men do not have the same abilities.

The parents' views reflect the reality of gender divisions of labour in agriculture. The majority of parents think that women are good at taking care of children, while only 15 (25 per cent) of them think that men can do this task well. Men are regarded as better at tasks connected with the practical work of the farm. In a class of their own, are the tasks of repairing the tractor and maintaining the farm, where men rank very high in comparison to women. Bookkeeping is considered to be more 'female' work, but this work is most commonly done by professional accountants and not by the farm couple themselves.

Table 5.2   Parents' views on how well women and men can perform tasks

	Parents' answers n and (%) saying 'well'	
	Women	Men
Feeding the cattle	51 (85)	55 (92)
Driving a harvester	33 (55)	53 (88)
Ploughing	34 (57)	53 (88)
Maintaining the farm	14 (23)	47 (78)
Bookkeeping	52 (87)	37 (61)
Repairing the tractor	11 (18)	47 (78)
Sowing	39 (65)	52 (86)
Taking care of small children	57 (95)	15 (25)

N = 60

Siblings and socialisation

Little light has been shed on the importance of the sibling relationship in gender socialisation, but there is reason to believe that farm girls with younger brothers are faced with different expectations (regarding the farm) from girls who do not have younger brothers or only younger sisters. A girl without brothers might be raised as the 'son' in order to maintain the farm within the family. The following quotation illustrates how Ruth regards the situation with younger siblings. She has many girlfriends who have the right of succession who all have younger brothers:

> Actually, it seems like it is taken for granted in many places that the girls do not want to have the farm, and that the boys are raised to be outside more. You see a different way of treating the children. I think you really have to work and be sure that you want to have the farm if you are a girl. At least I don't have to worry about that problem, because there are only girls in my family. But if there had been a boy, I think I would be very uncertain, probably, because I know – at least I think – that my father would rather have had a boy to take over. (Ruth, 19)

In our sample all but three of the girls had younger brother(s), and obviously the brother very often became a competitor regarding the succession of the farm. Berit is 18. She has taken a one-year course in agriculture and has worked at home on the farm during the past year. Berit would like to take over the farm, but so would her younger brother of 16. Berit says:

> When he gets to drive the tractor, he will do whatever you ask him. At school, when we went there it was always like – when anyone asked him what he wanted to be – he wanted to be a farmer when he grew up. But I have – I don't have any less interest, just because he does more on the farm. I don't think so.

When asked if anyone encourages her to take over, she answers; 'They haven't yet, at least. There hasn't been any talk about who is going to take over. We just do what we – we just do the work that has to be done.' Berit's father agrees with the law about allodial rights, but says that he wants his younger son to take over. Berit's mother encourages her to become a hair stylist, and says that it doesn't make any difference to her which child takes over.

Unni is 20 years old with a brother of 18. Their father does not agree with the law of allodial right, but says that he doesn't care which of his children takes over.

> We have discussed it a lot because my father is going to retire next year – but I think it will by my brother who takes over the farm. He is probably the one who has the greatest interest in it, and who is the most active. I think maybe they [her parents] want my brother to take over, too. They sort of see it as the son who actually has the right to take over the farm and pass it on to the next generations. They are sort of used to it being that way . . . I think it will be a little hard when he takes over the farm, in a way, because I have always been here, but I – in one way I don't really want to have it. But I think he does. He has always – it's sort of always been decided that he would take over the farm. We have talked about it that way, too. Not that I have been pressured – I haven't, but it has always been understood. (Unni, 20)

Unni is ambivalent towards the farm. The question whether to take over the farm or not could be seen as a moral dilemma. Unni has the first right to take over but at the same time, it has been *understood* that her brother would be the one to do so. Unni follows the 'ethic of care', evaluating her right in relationship to others. She knows that her parents would rather see her brother take over. She excuses her parents by saying they are used to it being that way. When her brother shows greater interest than she does, there is a legitimate explanation for why she will probably 'choose' not to exercise her right. She gives in fact higher value to the interests of others than to her own interest.

Agriculture has remained a male-dominated trade (Blekesaune, 1991), and it is reasonable to believe that a father's support of a daughter with the right of succession is important in her choice of making the farm her career. In our material, there are six girls who say that they are not planning to take over, and *none of the fathers* and only *one of the mothers* of these recommended that their daughters should use their allodial right. We can establish that those girls who say that they (probably) will not use their allodial right have not been encouraged to take over the farm.

The parents' opinion about the amendment of the law gives an indication of their attitude to girls in agriculture. The majority of the parents (66 per cent, N = 58) verbally agree in the amendment, while 22 per cent disagree and 12 per cent are ambivalent (see Table 5.3). It is possible to be for equality in principle, but evaluate the situation differently when it comes to one's own daughter inheriting. When parents were asked which of the children they *want* to take over the farm, it appears that parents of boys with the right to succession are more positive about their sons than parents of girls are about their daughters. While nearly half the parents of girls are indifferent as to which of the children takes

Table 5.3 Parents' opinion about the amendment of the law

	Parents of girls with right of succession n (%)		Parents of boys with right of succession n (%)		Mothers n (%)		Fathers n (%)	
Agree	27	(78)	11	(48)	20	(74)	18	(58)
Disagree	4	(11)	9	(39)	4	(15)	9	(29)
Ambivalent	4	(11)	3	(13)	3	(11)	4	(13)
Total	35	(100)	23	(100)	27	(100)	31	(100)

over the farm, nearly all the parents of boys want their sons to take over. We can conclude that boys are given more support than girls. In addition, there appears to be a discrepancy between the view of equality in principle and in practice in one's own family. If the principle of equality is considered to be in conflict with the parents' main goal of keeping the family farm intact, they seem to prioritise the second.

Role models for farmers' daughters

In the struggle to negotiate their identities as women *and* farmers, young girls might be expected to look to different role models: mothers, women farmers, women relief workers[6] and fathers. To the extent that such models are important, girls have few 'new' role models for their future careers as farmers. Mother's role on the farm is subordinate to father's; she has usually married into the farm, and her role is that of the farmer's wife rather than a farmer. In our material, all the fathers and none of the mothers had main responsibility for running the farm. More than half of the mothers were triple workers; they had off-farm work, usually on a part-time basis, while they also assisted in the work on the farm and had the main responsibility for domestic work. In spite of the fact that 10 per cent of Norwegian farmers are women – meaning solely or mainly responsible for the running of the farm (Haugen, 1990b) – very few of the girls knew any women farmers. Even where there were (married) women farmers in their neighbourhood, most commonly the girls referred to the male spouse as the farmer. This illustrates how invisible women are as farmers (Sachs, 1983).

Women relief workers appear to function as useful role models for girls. They have broken down many barriers and contributed to a change in many peoples' attitudes about women and agricultural work. A 16-year-old farmers' daughter describes them thus:

> We have had almost only women relief workers. We have had some men, too – we have had a lot of different ones over the years, but Papa thinks the women are at least as good as the men because the men are more careless. The women are conscientious. The first time he – or actually the group of farmers that hires the substitutes – was going to have a female substitute, they were not very keen on having a woman, but they were willing to try.

> And the one they took that time was the best substitute they have ever had. All the men were sceptical about having a female substitute, sort of, because they weren't so strong physically and couldn't do so much work . . . But the one we had first was really strong. She did everything they did and was really good. (Anne, 16)

The description of this woman relief worker is interesting. She is described as good because she is different from men (meaning better because she is more conscientious). At the same time she is like men (meaning she is just as strong and did the same work). When women do a better or at least as good a job as men, this can be an important step in changing people's attitudes. On the other hand the relief worker is employed to do a specific job, she (or he) is an assistant and not in a farmer's position. When young people consider the farm as a future place of work, the father's role as farmer is their main model. They consistently talk about the farmer as 'he', and when giving concrete examples, they use 'Father' in most every situation that has to do with farm work and farm management. No doubt this favours boys, because their occupational and gender model coincide. As we have seen, young girls have few female role models for their future as a farmer.

The paradox of choice

The young girls interviewed wanted to have an education, a career and a family. This is basically what the boys want too. But in contrast to the boys, the girls are the 'flexible' gender taking responsibility for combining these things. The girls will not choose to keep the farm at the expense of love; they will not choose a work situation that makes family life impossible. This may be one of the reasons for girls waiting longer than boys to decide whether or not they will take over the farm. If a girl is going to take over a farm, the choice of partner is relevant. It is significant, and often times decisive, for her to secure a partner who is interested in farming. Many parents say that they would recommend that the girl take over the farm *if* she finds a husband who is interested. We can interpret this in a positive way: that parents realise from their own experience that it takes two to run a farm. But we can also interpret this negatively – as a lack of confidence in girls' competence: parents believe that a woman needs a husband in order to be able to farm. The girls themselves regard common interests and support from their partners as important.

Neither the boys nor their parents say that finding a partner who is interested in farming is a necessary condition for a boy to take over the farm. Boys do not see this as a relevant problem. They assume they can have everything, and give priority to their own work and the farm. The boys expect their future wives to move on to the farm. If they don't, as one farmer's son put it:

> Well, then I would give up the woman before I would give up – I am going to have the farm. That's for sure. As I see it now, at least . . . We haven't made any definite plans, but I don't think it will be a problem. She'll just have to be a little flexible to accommodate for what I decide, I should think. (Erik, 20)

Erik follows the 'ethic of right', and he cannot see any reason to sacrifice his right even if his fiancé may not be happy about his decision. It is taken for granted that boys choose a career and a place to live independent of the interests that a future partner may have. The boys' attitudes are a hindrance to entering a relationship that gives equality to a woman's choice of career and residence. Statistics show an increasing percentage of elderly people in many rural communities, and the proportion of unmarried young men is increasing (25 per cent of male farmers under 40 years are single). This will probably be a growing problem in the future, both for the individual and for rural society in general.

Some of the girls have already established relationships with boys who have rights to succession and find themselves with a moral dilemma. Ruth is engaged to a boy who is to take over his parents' farm, and they have decided that is the farm they will take over. She has two younger sisters, but neither has shown any special interest in the farm. Ruth feels that she has the responsibility to carry on the tradition of the family farm and that she therefore has betrayed her parents since she will not be taking over her home farm. This is how she explains why they have to choose her financé's farm:

> I feel like I'm being drawn in two directions – I ought to be both places. I feel that Lars has to make the decision, because he has, after all, grown up there, and I can't do very much outside [because of allergies – my comment]. But he knows that I would just as soon live here. The location of our farm is better, really, down by the sea, much freer than up there right by a road with a lot of traffic. So for children growing up, I would say it is much better here. (Ruth, 19)

Ruth maintains the impression of having a free choice. She points out good reasons for choosing the husband's farm, even though she feels tied to her home farm. Ruth follows the traditional patrilocal pattern in agriculture; women move to their husbands' family farm. Girls are willing to give up their home farms for the sake of 'love', while the boys would not consider doing so. This can be understood as an illustration of women's subordination; and even a concealing of this subordination by the women themselves by giving plausible explanations for why the choices must be the way they are.

Even though today we have (formal) equality for both sexes with respect to taking over the family farm, there remains a discrepancy between theory and practice. This appears in a variety of ways; through different expectations between girls and boys, through attitudes and practice. The challenges girls face are in many ways greater than previously; they are expected to solve the dilemma between ideology and practice. Equality has focused on getting women to change their choices and choose like men, while men can continue as they have done. Reidun expresses it in her own words:

> I think it's a little strange, too, in a way that it's always 'girls should do that, and should do this and that and that,' but there's never anything about what boys should be doing. For them it's sort of a matter of course . . . . It's like that with all careers, it seems like, with equality, that girls have to start there and there and there, and try something untraditional. If

you want to try something traditional, that's wrong, it seems. But boys are just supposed to do what they want to. You don't see any posters around saying 'Be a househusband and apply to a school for homemakers. Boys can do it, too!' You never see that, do you? Everyone knows the pay is poor, so they better not move the boys down in that direction. (Reidun, 19)

Girls are careful about making responsible decisions. If their own interests come in conflict with those of others, they are more ready to make a sacrifice, than to expect it of someone else. This way of thinking responsibly, that marks the modern farm woman's life project, makes freedom of choice paradoxical. Compared to her mother, today's farm girl has more opportunities, both within and outside agriculture. But while girls now have a 'choice', they also have more responsibility for their own project for equality in a society which is still marked by a gender system that subordinates women's interests.

The lessons from Norway

The young women in this study represent the first generation of women who have obtained formal equality of rights with men to take over their parents' farm. In future this will probably be the most important source of recruitment for women into agriculture, replacing marriage. Marrying a farmer will no longer automatically mean their involvement in farm work. If agriculture doesn't succeed in recruiting this new generation of women, the farm work will in future be even more masculinised (Blekesaune *et al.,* 1993).

The study has shown that legislation for women's rights, doesn't automatically change women's lived experience. Even where the law regulating succession to a farm is 'gender neutral', we still find an 'ideological lag' in agriculture. Not all parents want to stand behind the idea of equality as presented in the amendment to the law concerning the right of succession. The fact that exercising their allodial rights is a very difficult decision for many girls, is largely due to the gendered expectations, attitudes and practices they meet in their daily lives. Even when girls receive the practical training necessary to become farmers, their socialisation still centres on constructions of womanhood as a flexible and caring gender. While the question of taking over the farm is, for girls, an evaluation of many conditions in which other people's interests play an important part, boys evaluate the situation according to their own personal interests. The life project of women would appear to be more difficult and complicated than the more unidimensional and career-oriented project typical of men.

It is clear that a state policy of equality and amendments to the law is not sufficient to alter the gendered structure of social relations in agriculture, although they may constitute a necessary first step. This is likely to be even more true in countries where the agricultural culture is less influenced by state policy, such as southern Europe and Ireland. However, we can see that the policy of equality has already succeeded in getting the agricultural population to accept gender equality at least in theory. The farmers' organisations, which in 1974 were working against the amendment, are now supporting campaigns to inform their membership about the amendment and encourage young women to use their rights. Gender issues are now on the agenda. There is still insufficient work on this to sustain significant change on the ground. The aspirations of young girls and boys are shaped most strongly by their everyday experiences on the farm and in their communities. A combination of efforts on the macro and micro level would seem to be necessary to affect change. A macro-level state policy based on gender equality marks a beginning, and will eventually contribute to a change of practice at the local level. If three out of ten girls in future will use their allodial right, this in itself will raise the portion of women farmers in Norway and, in this way, hopefully promote more significant changes in attitude towards women and farming. Women's formal (juridical) status is today equal with that of men but, as this study has shown, the most important negotiations and decisions have to be made in households and communities, and not in courts.

Notes

1. This list is by no means complete.
2. Bradley's (1989) definition of sex-typing is 'the process by which jobs are "gendered", ascribed to one sex or the other' (p. 9).
3. A growing body of feminist literature deals with the issue of women and property both historically and cross-culturally (Hirschon, 1984; Whitehead, 1984; Salmon, 1986; Salamon and Davis-Brown, 1988).
4. Thorsen (1993) uses the term to describe farm women in Norway.
5. The reason for studying heirs with younger siblings was that those heirs had, at least in theory, several choices. If they did not want to exercise their allodial rights themselves, one of the younger siblings could carry on the family farm. At the same time, having younger siblings implies potential competition for the farm.
6. Relief workers are wage workers employed by a group of farmers. The farmers use relief workers during holidays, weekends and when the farmer is sick. The state subsidises the wages to the relief workers to secure farmers' time off.

References

Almaas, R., Vik, K. and Oedegaard, J. (1983) Women in rural Norway. Recent tendencies in the development of the division of labour in agriculture and participation of rural women on the labour market. SFB-paper 83: 1. Trondheim, Centre for Rural Research.

Bjerrum Nielsen, H. and Rudberg, M. (1989) *Historien om jenter og gutter. Kjønnssosialsering i et utviklingspsykologisk perspektiv.* Oslo, Universitetsforlaget.

Blekesaune, A. (1991) Changes in ways of making a living among Norwegian farmers 1975–1990. *Sociologia Ruralis,* 1: 48–57.

Blekesaune, A., Haney, W.G. and Haugen, M.S. (1993) On the question of the feminisation of production on part-time farms: evidence from Norway. *Rural Sociology,* 1: 111–29.

Bouquet, M. and de Haan, H. (1987) Kinship as an analytical category in rural sociology. An introduction. *Sociologia Ruralis,* 3: 243–62.

Bradley, H. (1989) *Men's Work, Women's Work.* Oxford, Polity Press.

Gasson, R., Crow, G., Errington, A., Hutson, J., Marsden, T. and Winter, D.M. (1988) The farm as a family business: a review. *Journal of Agricultural Economics,* 39: 1–41.

Gilligan, C. (1982) *In a Different Voice: Essays on Psychological Theory and Women's Development.* Cambridge, Mass., Harvard University Press.

Haavind, H. (1992) Kvinners utviklingsmuligheter i en verden i forandring. In *Kjønnsidentitet, utvikling og konstruksjon av kjønn:* 27–64. Skriftserie 1, Trondheim, Centre for Women's Studies.

Hacker, S.A. (1979) Sex stratification, technology and organisational change: a longitudinal case study at AT & T. *Social Problems,* 26: 539–57.

Harding, S. (1986) *The Science Question in Feminism.* Ithaca, Cornell University Press.

Haugen, M.S. (1990a) Female farmers in Norwegan agriculture. From traditional farm women to professional farmers. *Sociologia Ruralis,* 2: 197–209.

Haugen, M.S. (1990b) *Kvinnebonden,* SFB-rapport 90: 7. Trondheim, Centre for Rural Research.

Hirschon, R. (1984) (ed.) *Women and Property – Women as Property.* New York, St Martin's Press.

Hirschon, R. (1984) Property, power and gender relations. In Hirschon, R. (ed.) *Women and Property – Women as Property.* New York, St Martin's Press.

Johnsen, M. (1986) Faktorer som kan påvirke odelsjentenes bruk av odelsretten. Hovedfagsoppgave ved Institutt for landbruks-konomi, AS–NLH.

Noddings, N. (1984) *Caring – A Feminist Approach to Ethics and Moral Education.* Berkeley, University of California Press.

Ølnes, A. (1989) *Odelsjenter, barrierer og muligheter.* SFB-rapport, 89: 1. Trondheim, Centre for Rural Research.

Potter, C. and Lobley, M. (1992) Ageing and succession on family farms: the impact on decision-making and land use. *Sociologia Ruralis,* XXXII(2/3): 317–34.

Prokop, U. (1981) *Kvinnors livssammanhang: begrænsade strategier och omättliga önskninger.* Stockholm, Raben and Sjögren.

Sachs, C.E. (1983) *The Invisible Farmers. Women in Agricultural Production.* Tatowa, New Jersey, Rowan and Allanheld.

Salamon, S. and Davis-Brown, K. (1988) Farm continuity and female land inheritance: a family dilemma. In Haney, W.G. and Knowles, J.B. (eds) *Women and Farming, Changing Roles, Changing Structures.* Boulder and London, Westview Press.

Salamon, S. and Keim, A.M. (1979) Land ownership and women's power in a Midwestern farming community. *Journal of Marriage and the Family,* 41: 109–19.

Salmon, M. (1986) *Women and the Law of Property in Early America.* Chapel Hill, The University of North Carolina Press.

Shortall, S. (1992) Power analysis and farm wives: an empirical study of the power relationships affecting women on Irish farms. *Sociologia Ruralis,* 4: 431–51.

Sørensen, B.Aa. (1982) Ansvarsrasjonalitet: om mål – middeltenkning blant kvinner. In Holter, H. (ed.) *Kvinner i fellesskap,* s. 392–402. Oslo, Universitetsforlaget.

Symes, D. (1990) Bridging the generations: succession and inheritance in a changing world. *Sociologia Ruralis,* 3/4: 280–91.

Thorsen, L.E. (1993) *Det fleksible kjønn. Mentalitetsendringer i tre generasjoners bondekvinner 1920–1985.* Oslo, Universitetsforlaget.

West, C. and Zimmermann, D.H. (1991) Doing gender. In Lorber, J. and Farell, S.A. *The Social Construction of Gender:* 13–37. Newbury Park, Sage Publications.

Whatmore, S. (1991) *Farming Women. Gender, Work and Family Enterprise.* London, Macmillan.

Whitehead, A. (1984) Men and women, kinship and property: some general issues. In Hirschon, R. (ed.) *Women and Property – Women as Property.* New York, St Martin's Press.

CHAPTER 6

Women Farmers and the Influence of Ecofeminism on the Greening of German Agriculture

Mathilde Schmitt

Introduction

The dynamics of rural change give occasion for continuous exploration and re-interpretation. But much research still does not take into account that social change is differently experienced by women, and causes other consequences for them, than for men. Either 'gender' is still not being used as a structural category in investigations, or women's experiences are ignored. In agriculture for instance women experience different agencies and possibilities to create their surroundings if they want to do the same job as men, to manage a farm. Women's decisions in matters such as these influence social change in agriculture in a specific way which needs to be addressed directly.

As in other EC countries, agriculture in Germany has been characterised by an intensifying process of restructuring. Besides the GATT negotiations in 1992, this process was accelerated by German re-unification in 1989. Another less appreciated aspect of change is the increasing number of farmers practising ecological farming. Still less than 1 per cent, besides Denmark Germany has the highest proportion of organic and biodynamic farms and ecologically farmed land area in the EC (Lampkin, 1993: 11). The official agricultural statistics (Agrarbericht, 1993; Agöl, 1993) show the increase given in Table 6.1.

This development was supported by the Green Party's entry into parliament (in 1981 they managed to win seats in the Hessian Parliament and in 1983 in the Federal Parliament) and their efforts to bring ecological principles more

Table 6.1

	Organic and biodynamic farms	Area which is farmed in an ecological way
1980	579	some 11,000 ha
1985	1,452	some 25,000 ha
1992	4,385	127,240 ha

into the political agenda. In addition to the risks of nuclear power, the destructive impact of acid rain on German forests and other environmental topics, they drew attention to the damage to the environment from industrialised agriculture. The support of sustainable environmentally sound farming was an important part of their political programme. After many years of struggle they met with success in 1989 in agricultural politics: Germany became the first country of the EC to support organic and biodynamic farming within land extensification programmes.

The women of the Green Party who discussed ecological problems in the context of social and economic conditions and women's subordination influenced these discussions in a number of ways. One of the important personalities of this time was Petra Kelly. In her opinion feminism, freedom from violence and ecology belong together:

> They are strongly connected. All three movements deal with a completely different kind of power, namely: the abolition of power, which we experience and suffer today. 'Power over' has to be replaced by shared power, the power to do things from the bottom, the discovery of our own power in contrast to a passive acceptance of power. (Kelly, 1987: 21)

The significance of ecofeminist thinking and practice within this movement also became apparent at the congress 'Women and Ecology. Disillusionment with Omnipotence' (Frauen und Okologie. Wider den Machbarkeitswahn). This was organised from the 3rd to the 5th October 1986, by the working group of the parliamentary Green Party called 'Women's Politics'. The assembly and the discussions of 800 women on the topic 'women and ecology' was a political signal of women's changed demands. In the 1970s and 1980s a number of German women had begun to think of other ways of making a living than was conventional. They summoned up courage to pioneer new paths for themselves and to lay claim to them for other women.

In the rural areas one way in which this movement was manifested took the form of women laying claim to the status of farmer, a still predominantly male-defined occupation, and, thereby, calling into question the traditional relationship between men and women in agriculture. These women farmers have consciously chosen agriculture as a professional career; have done an apprenticeship in practical farming or attended an agricultural university; are familiar with all the technological farm equipment and operations; and totally involved in day-to-day farm work. They are the sole or main operators of the farms and can best be described as professional female farmers.[1]

The increased number of young women managing a farm in the last 20 years can only be understood in context of the wider women's liberation movement. The extent to which German women farmers have been influenced by ecofeminist ideas is the central question addressed in this paper. Firstly, I will sketch the theory of ecofeminism as it has been elaborated in Germany and consider its influence in agricultural pressure groups. The rest of the paper then uses the results of field research conducted in the 1990s to analyse the significance of ecofeminism as an influence on the ideas and practices of professional female farmers in German agriculture.[2]

German ecofeminism

In examining the relationship between ecofeminist theory and women farmers who use nature and assist nature in reproducing natural goods in everyday life, I want to concentrate on two key points of ecofeminist disussion in Germany: firstly, the relationship between the subordination of women and the exploitation of nature in contemporary industrial capitalist society; and secondly, the devaluation of reproductive work associated with human and other life processes.

The subordination of women and nature has been supported by the development of 'objective' natural science since the Age of Enlightenment. Nowadays most people's understanding of nature is influenced by the 'objective' natural sciences and technology, which are taught at our schools and universities. Feminist natural scientists were the first to make public that this understanding is influenced by masculine perspectives and men's social experiences. The 'objectivity' of natural science and technology is not fact but illusion.

> First the natural scientists project their subjective social experiences and values on nature, see it as objective, according to the dominant ideology and then they authorise the hierarchical, exploitative patriarchal society with this patriarchal picture of nature as 'natural'.[3] (Jansen, 1984: 72)

According to Elvira Scheich this attitude is maintained through the splitting of different spheres of life and the rigid categorisation of behavioural characteristics as specifically male or female, which is significant for a domineering and exploitative use of nature by scientists, but also by farmers. By splitting responsibility competence, 'according to the division of labour acknowledgement is reduced to an objectivity of the lack of relationship to the real world . . . the part of "love" is passed to the women, who adopt this' (Scheich, 1987: 93f), the environment is objectified, so that it can be taken and used as men's own – if necessary by force.

For women it is difficult to 're-appropriate' technology, science, power and acknowledgement, as these characteristics are composed in contrast to feminity, affinity, care and dependence, which confront them with contradictions. They are challenged to live with and to withstand these contradictions, because 'our ideas and models of another science, another gender relationship, another kind of power cannot be separated from our experiences and possibility of experiencing' (Scheich, 1987: 98).

In Erika Hickel's view women and their experience have to be integrated into the scientific community and men have to be forced to share *all* spheres of everyday life 'that they learn to integrate everyday life into their research life' (Hickel, 1987: 111), otherwise our society will not develop a re-orientation of natural science and a use of nature, which is adequate. This already refers to the important meaning of reproductive work in the ecofeminist discussion. Besides the fact that men don't have a share in these tasks, the second reason for women's subordination in this society is seen in the devaluation of subsistence work.

Veronika Bennholdt-Thomsen speaks of the 'de-economisation of subsistence production' (Bennholdt-Thomsen, 1989: 121). The financial economy must extinguish the knowledge of another economy, which is mostly maintained by women, 'because the domination of artificial products, the capitalist financial and goods economy can only function by denial, violent separation and the hushing up of natural productivity' (Bennholdt-Thomsen, 1989: 125). The devaluation of women belongs to this and vice versa 'an appreciation of women without insult and degradation is connected to the social restoration of subsistence production' (Bennholdt-Thomsen 1989: 121) and *not* to the equal participation in the capitalist financial and goods economy. Women 'will never get the same appreciation as men in this context, because accumulation, ecological destruction and the political system are held together by an important "clip": sexism' (Bennholdt-Thomsen, 1987: 33).

In contrast to this argument Ilse Lenz stresses the urgency of various kinds of women's resistance to enable the development of a self-determined future for women with equal rights and freedom from oppression and exploitation. In her opinion subsistence production should not remain 'female' because the split responsibility for life, allocated to women, and death, allocated to men, makes subsistence production exploitative. She speaks of the 'historical scandal, that fathers refuse to take the responsibility of parental care, and all its destructive consequences' (Lenz, 1988: 172).

In 1983 Maria Mies had already argued together with Veronika Bennholdt-Thomsen and Claudia von Werlhof, 'that sexism and patriarchy are not signs of backwardness, but important ideological and institutional parts of the industrial system and its model of accumulation' (Werlhof *et al.,* 1983: 5) and that 'it is not possible to think of the labourer, who is free in a double sense, without thinking of the house-wife, the unfree, wageless, dependent, minor female worker' (Werlhof, *et al.,* 1983: 10). They have reproached the representatives of the environmental and alternative movements for systematically screening out of their social analyses and projects 'the invisible, supporting foundations of society: the women and the colonies or the underdeveloped societies' (Werlhof, *et al.,* 1983: 3).

Based on these analyses Maria Mies has developed a concept of liberation the main principle of which is to reject development, or liberation, by exploitation and violence against nature, women and racialised peoples. Other principles are to reproduce reciprocal, non-hierarchical social relations and to reject hierarchical and dualistic separations. The limitations of our reality also need to be appreciated. Where no infinite progress or growth can exist we need to find another way of defining happiness, freedom and human necessities in a finite world. She sees regional subsistence economies as a necessary basis for developing these principles. According to Maria Mies, in such a society it is easier to achieve the aims of the womens' liberation movement – such as suspending the division of work by hierarchy or gender; putting the means of subsistence at women's disposal; giving the women autonomy over their body – presupposing the disarmament and demilitarisation of men.

Maria Mies suggests that women renounce their 'complicity' with the patriarchal system and politicise everyday life as a way of realising these utopian ideas. In her opinion an effective strategy would be to politicise consumption and establish a consumption liberation movement. This would disrupt the capitalist-patriarchal system and also make people more conscious of real human needs. Through such a strategy, she argues, some autonomy could be regained. In addition, it would be important to support all kinds of struggles and movements for overcoming exploitative industrial systems, for instance producer-consumer groups, campaigns against concentrated feed imports from the Third World, against the politics of the chemical industry, and against gene and reproduction technologies.

Ilse Lenz' key question with respect to this vision of 'ambivalent technology' is 'how can nature be "appropriated" without domination so that human work can be eased whilst taking humen and natural cycles into consideration to overcome the classical industrial society with its destructive character' (Lenz, 1987: 73). In contrast to Maria Mies, Ilse Lenz stresses the necessity of:

> politics as the central sphere of change: one cannot imagine an ecological conversion of production and needs without women's freedom to intervene, to suggest and to use their power. This is not desirable either, because without general freedom it would be a dictatorship over human needs. (Lenz, 1987: 74)

According to Ilse Lenz the necessity of everybody's self-determination and of political democratic decision-making also exists in regional economic structures, a point which is missing from Maria Mies' utopian scheme of an ecofeminist society.

Ecofeminism and agricultural politics

I now want to turn to some political and pressure groups in which ecofeminist ideas have been introduced and found practical responses. Even if the model of an ecofeminist society has not found a sympathetic hearing with the majority of the green politicians, their discussions and political manoeuvres have none the less been stimulated by ecofeminist ideas. Women members of the Green Party involved in the congress 'Women and Ecology', discussed earlier, together with the above-mentioned representatives of ecofeminism and other feminist scientists and politicians, have been active contributors of ideas within the wider debates of the Green Party. Maria Mies' first attempt to define a utopian scheme of an ecofeminist society was made together with a group of autonomous and 'green' women in 1983 (Mies, 1988: 302). The close contact between 'green' women politicians, ecofeminist scientists and grass-roots women generated new ideas and brought them into the public arena, including debates in parliament.

An organisation which was open-minded towards ecofeminist ideas was the 'Agrarian Alliance' (Agrarbündnis) which was founded by the merging of 13 different organisations with a total of about 1 million members in 1988 to fight and campaign for an environmentally and socially sound peasant agriculture; a re-orientation of agricultural politics; an adequate rural infrastructure; equal rights for rural women and solidarity with the people in the Third World (Agrarbündnis, 1993: 8). Here one can find the greatest congruences between ecofeminism and other agro-environmental interests. This being said, it should be noted that this alliance was still characterised by a marked lack of women's participation in its decision-making bodies. Ecofeminist ideas were also viewed with interest by the AbL (Arbeitsgemeinschaft bäverliche Landwirtschaft), a pressure group for peasant agriculture, which defines itself as the agrarian opposition to the official farmers' union. Parallels between ecofeminism and the aims of AbL can be found in the areas of ecology, Third World issues and support of regional economic integrity based on small-scale networks. On the other hand opinions were divided on the question of feminist demands for women's rights which many of the male members of the AbL found unacceptable. Only for moderate women's demands could the organisation find a consensus. As a consequence they have concentrated, along with other groups (e.g. the Green Party and the 'Agrarian Alliance') on campaigning for equal social rights for farmers' wives. They managed to bring this important topic into discussion at many political levels.

Congruences between ecofeminism and political, as well as pressure, groups have largely been explored for the purposes of specific interests and aims. Debates about political strategy and practice within such groups have been stimulated by ecofeminist ideas, but the model of an ecofeminist society in its totality has not been taken up by any of these groups. As Marieluise Beck-Oberdorf, member of the Green Party, argued, a major reason for this lies in the fact that this model 'does not offer practical political possibilities' (Beck-Oberdorf, 1987: 140). New ideas are evaluated to see if they are workable or not, and perhaps this is, in any case, the proper function of utopian schemes – to deconstruct established ways of thinking and to suggest new possibilities. In this more diffuse sense, ecofeminist ideas and politics can be seen to be manifested through their influence on women farmers.

Ecofeminism and professional female farmers

Ecofeminism has connected feminist ideas and strategies with ecological ones. The ecological influences on professional female farmers can be seen in the

Table 6.2 Farm managers of the former FRG in 1991 according to age

Age	Total number	Percentage of women
15–24	10,900	14.2
25–34	87,200	8.3
35–44	139,000	6.7
45–54	166,300	6.3
55–64	172,800	6.5
>65	41,800	22.8
Total	618,000	8.0

(*Source*: Agrarbericht, 1992)

realisation of organic or biodynamic farming practices; the feminist influences in their demand for a self-determined way of making a living in agriculture founded on apprenticeship.

The number of women undertaking an apprenticeship to be a farmer increased from 1.3 per cent of all agricultural pupils in 1978 to 5.2 per cent in 1982 (Riechel, 1983: 15) to around 8 per cent in 1992 (Lauter, 1992). Among young people the percentage of women managing a farm is also higher than among older people (see Table 6.2).

In the absence of any official statistics to show the number of women working on, or managing, ecological farms, I sought to gain information by placing an advertisement in 25 agricultural magazines and newspapers, publicising my research on professional female farmers in West Germany. Seventy women farmers responded from all over Western Germany. Their responses included replies to save basic questions about their socio-economic characteristics; such as age, marital status, professional education, farm characteristics etc., which made possible a systematic collection of data according to the principles of Grounded Theory (Glaeser and Strauss, 1967; Strauss and Corbin, 1990). Participant observation is being undertaken to supplement this background data in combination with interviews and a questionnaire-based survey. The research is still in progress, so that the statements and arguments about women farmers contained in the following pages represent a preliminary analysis of results so far.

If women decide to become professional farmers they choose what is still a definitively masculine occupational status in farming. Even though they are well aware of this, the extent to which the masculine definition of these activities exists, and its consequences for women, only become apparent after the first few years of farming. At the beginning, some women are driven by an overriding interest in the skills and techniques of farming and are confident that 'being a woman will be irrelevant to their work' (Brandth and Bolsø, 1991: 6). Others feel challenged to conquer those spheres of farming from which women have traditionally been excluded.

Both these attitudes were evident amongst the women farmers with whom I have been in contact.

As they [the male teachers] always let me know, I shouldn't imagine that they would be indulgent towards me as a woman; I really got angry and I swore 'I will show them that I am as good as a man'. (AR, 93)[4]

Quite often the women developed this attitude during their apprenticeship, because they had to experience a lot of prejudice and lack of recognition of their abilities from men.

For women who farm like this it means following a 'male' model of farming as it has been developed in the industrialised Western societies where economic priorities are overriding. They do not call into question either the value attached to male work or its intention and consequences for society or nature. These women use their competence and influence to have a share of the agricultural 'booty' with all its consequences: increasing problems of soil erosion, water pollution, resistant plant pests and decreasing animal fertility. Until very recently, this kind of agriculture has dominated the curricula taught at agricultural schools and universities.

The majority of the 70 women farmers who answered my advertisement farm in this conventional way (see Table 6.3).

Table 6.3 Organic orientation of surveyed women farmers

Way of farming	Women farmers
Conventional	54 = 77%
Organic/biodynamic	16 = 23%

The ratio of organic/biodynamic women farmers to conventional women farmers is 1:4. This differs markedly from the official statistical ratio of organic/biodynamic to conventional farms which is 1:99. In Germany there are about 601,000 farms but only 4,385 (0.7 per cent) of them practice ecological methods (Agrarbericht, 1993; Agöl, 1993). The percentage of young women in my sample is higher than in the official statistics. It might be reasonable to expect this ecological bias to be affected by age. As there are no official statistics to show the age and gender of German organic/biodynamic farmers, I will refer to a questionnaire-based survey of 148 farmers in Baden-Württemberg in southern Germany, who re-organised conventional production in 1989/90, and compare these results with mine.

In comparison with the total number of farmers in the former FRG or in Baden-Württemberg the average age of farmers in the process of transition to ecological farming is much lower. The tendency of preferring organic or biodynamic farming is much higher in farmers aged 35 or younger. But the percentage of organic or biodynamic professional female farmers of this age group is even higher. Even if the different data do not allow an exact comparison, it shows women's tendency to prefer organic or biodynamic farming, if they enter agriculture as professional farmers (see Table 6.4).

In what ways do ecological women farmers develop their power to realise an environmentally and socially sound agriculture? Farmers' daughters who take over their parents' farm, or rented them, first have to convert conventional

110

Table 6.4 Age and gender distribution of organic farmers

Age	Baden-Württemberg	Farmers in transition	Former FRG Totally	Women farmers Totally	Eco-farming
	Totally				
<35	13.8%	46.5%	15.9%	64.3%	81.0%
35–55	46.7%	47.4%	49.4%	30.0%	19.0%
>55	39.5%	6.1%	34.7%	5.7%	0.0%
	100.0%	100.0%	100.0%	100.0%	100.0%

(*Source:* Agrarbericht, 1993; Dabbert and Braun, 1993; own results)

production as far as they are allowed to. In my sample seven of the sixteen women who practise ecological farming, have already made the conversion even though a few of them experienced serious differences of opinion with their parents because of this. Another four, who are still farming conventionally with their parents, told me they would prefer ecological farming but have not yet been able to persuade their parents. 'My father wouldn't rent me the farm if I changed the way of farming' (AH, 47). The other nine ecological women farmers do not have an agricultural background. Influenced by the environmental movement they were engaged in different working, pressure or producer–consumer groups and gradually developed the desire to work more closely with nature in everyday life. As there were not enough apprenticeships on organic or biodynamic farms at this time a few of them were forced to take one on a conventional farm, yet they were convinced that ecological farming would be the option they would choose when in a position to do so. They usually managed to do this with a rented farm or as a member of a farming group.

What about the representation of women in organic/bio-dynamic agriculture and its organisations? The percentage of women in committees, in consultant and managing positions of organic/biodynamic farm organisations is slightly higher than in conventional ones. Equal representation is a formulated aim, but it is still far off (Bioland, 1989).

> Actually I did not want to be a group leader. As all the members, whose competence I appreciated, did not accept this function I said yes when I was asked. At the regional meeting once again I will be the only woman but meanwhile I have got used to it. (AN, 59)

According to ecofeminist principles, dealing with nature and other people in a reciprocal way is part of ecological women farmers' ideology. It also includes farming without the exploitation of nature and the Third World. The women farmers' arguments for ecological farming are centred on being closer to nature; producing crops in a natural way without artificial fertilizers and pesticides; appreciating animals as living beings; having a broad food self-sufficiency; and working in a self-determined way. But the demands of ecological women farmers are often in conflict with the prevailing structures of patriarchal capitalist society and they have to face persistent contradictions between ecology and economy, and between productive and reproductive work on the farm. In the next section I will show how ecological women farmers try to 'appropriate' nature 'without domination so that human work can be eased whilst taking human and natural cycles into consideration' (Lenz, 1987: 73), and how they experience handling the daily reproductive work.

Contradictions for ecological women farmers

Humans cannot exist without healthy soil where healthy plants and animals can grow and live. Ecological women farmers' main task in their dealings with nature is to care for the soil, especially if they take over fields which received little attentive care before. The required work does not immediately succeed in producing economic results but is undertaken on a long-term basis. Such a behaviour conflicts with our fast-living, market-orientated society. The motivation to do it is nourished by the women's insight into, and their knowledge of, natural life cycles. In contrast to the short time span of productive and profitable criteria, ecological women farmers try with environmentally conscious approaches to re-build the soil of fields which have been damaged by erosion or by using large machinery when the weather was unfavourable.

> Actually I am proud that there is no erosion this year even on the steepest fields. It has given me trouble for over three years. Friends already said I should leave it, that it wouldn't be worthwhile, that it wouldn't be profitable. (AN, 72)

Besides the time and energy spent on such activities, it is important to buy and use machinery which suits the natural conditions of the farm well. As ecological women farmers strive for farming methods which preserve natural resources, they do not want to use technology which wastes natural resources. With many new technological developments on the market, ecological women farmers are challenged when considering which is best for their purposes; when setting ecological aims against the easing of daily work; and when deciding to buy this or that new technology.

> Sometimes it's not easy to know what's the right thing to do. As it is getting harder to sell your products your thoughts are occupied with economic considerations. I consciously have to remind myself what's my actual aim. (AF, 91)

Almost every day the reflections of organic or biodynamic women farmers move between ecological and economic arguments and they have to find a compromise, which 'connects the quality of production with good working conditions' (Bioland, 1989: 5). A number of women in my sample do this by buying used farm machinery and improving details; for instance a new comfortable, well-cushioned seat, which is good for their health. Women especially appreciate the easing of work by technology not least because they are not, on average, as physically strong as men. The 'opportunity' for women to handle farm machinery successfully on their own has increased, even though machinery design still assumes a male physique and many small things could be improved; for instance adjustable levers on tractors or farm machinery according to height.

The second contradictory question for ecological women farmers is: who does the necessary subsistence work on their farms? It is a question of more importance on organic or biodynamic farms because there is usually a greater amount of subsistence work on farms like these. The different opinions of feminist scholars on this topic (re-distribution or re-valuation) can be seen in discussions between ecological women farmers and their husbands or male partners in farming groups. On the one hand, professional women farmers are qualified for farm work, on the other hand, as women they experience social pressures to assume responsibilities for domestic work. They have to face strong conflict between these two spheres of work. Women who live and/or work with men constitute 76 per cent of my sample.

At the beginning of every private and/or working partnership there is a tendency for men and women to participate in caring for children, doing housework and working in the garden to almost the same extent.

> In the beginning it was very important to me that we equally divided the housework and that he prepared the meal at least twice a week even if it was a big effort for him and he needed twice as long as I to do it. (AN, 26)

But after a while this changes. Quite often the women do not enjoy continually having to remind men about their equal participation. They are forced to look for a way between the traditional women's work which is undervalued and the professional farm work which is appreciated. Particularly if they have small children, they end up taking over a lot of the subsistence work. In different cases I was able to observe the women's change of strategy: they now emphasise the importance of subsistence work for the farm and its functioning and demand that men at least appreciate this. If the men do so, a few of the ecological women farmers even experience the change and broader variety of jobs in the field, the farmyard and the farmhouse positively.

> I realised that it was not so important to me that we both did the same, e.g. that he also cooked but that he is aware of cooking as essential work. Then it's even good to leave field work at 11 o'clock and go home to prepare the meal. (AN, 26)

More appreciation for subsistence work is given on farms where only women live. But the same happens everywhere when the farm work load increases: domestic work is neglected.

The close proximity and the possibility of interlocking productive and reproductive work is still particular to agriculture and could be a starting-point for realising ecofeminist utopian schemes. Nowadays it seems possible only with an extreme work load, or even self-exploitation of the women farmers, if it is not possible to integrate as many working people as needed. If the women farm with their parents, quite often their mothers are responsible for doing the housework and the cooking: 'Fortunately my mother does all this work' (UW,

35); 'That's not my business, I don't like it. When my mother isn't able to do it any longer I will hire a housekeeper' (RG, 44). A few of the women farmers decided to hire somebody for several hours a week to clean up the house: 'I enjoy having clean windows, floors and so on, but I am not willing to use my spare time on it. Up to now I can afford to hire a cleaner' (HJ, 78). This is the result of being part of the capitalist system where agriculture is a business and not a way of living. In spite of the greater importance of subsistence work in farm households than in others, it seems to me that an autonomy, in the sense of Veronika Bennholdt-Thomsen, can only be achieved if women concentrate only on subsistence production and not if they try to combine it with professional market-orientated farm work. Like employed women in other economic areas, ecological women farmers experience the same dilemmas of a 'double burden'.

Conclusions

Professional women farmers are initiators of rural change. If women work professionally in agriculture they prefer organic or biodynamic farming to a higher degree than men. As they also claim a self-determined and legally independent role on the farm, they are potential practitioners of ecofeminist ideas. Ecofeminism is a concept of liberation without exploitation and violence against nature, women and racialised peoples. The realisation of this utopian scheme contradicts the social conditions of capitalist patriarchal society, but still initiates impulses for change. Accordingly, ecological women farmers experience contradictions and resistance if they challenge the conventional social order on the farm and realise their ideas of an environmentally sound agriculture in their everyday life.

The women's liberation and the environmental movements of the 1970s and the 1980s have prepared and facilitated such a way of life for women. The Green Party caught on to these topics and brought them to parliament, where they influenced the discussions and declarations both for socially and environmentally sound agricultural politics and equal rights for women. One of the consequences in agriculture has been the financial help for organic and biodynamic farming as part of the extensification programmes of different German states. It is now succeeding with the financial help of the conversion from conventional to ecological farming as part of the EC-extensification programme which started in 1993. This can be seen as the first step in a change of mind towards accepting that we can no longer afford an agriculture based on the exploitation of natural resources, if its long-term sustainability is to be secured.

The two other principles of ecofeminism, liberation without exploitation of women and of racialised peoples, have been manifested in campaigns for equal social security for farmers' wives and against the import of concentrated feed from countries of the Third World initiated by agricultural pressure groups all over the EC. The consequences for the social structure which are caused by these changed conditions, such as refashioned gender relationships with new defined gender roles, have still to make an impression, even if the percentage of women who do an apprenticeship in agriculture and manage a farm increases or at least stays constant.

These new, but established developments should not be ignored by rural sociologists in their research on rural change or the future of agriculture. The question of family farming has to be investigated in a new way if women are the professional managers of the farm, and new questions asked about the conventional division of farm and house work. Environmental issues have to be considered as integral to rural development more broadly. It would be very interesting to know if the tendency towards an increased preference for organic and biodynamic farming in young farmers, both male and female, shown here can be found more conclusively for Germany as a whole, and for other European countries. To this end, it is vital that the 'age' and 'gender' of participants in agriculture became a consistent feature of agricultural statistics and investigations of rural change, so that researchers are better able to draw a more differentiated picture of rural realities and trajectories.

Notes

The author wishes to thank Sarah Whatmore for valuable editorial suggestions.
1. This definition was inspired by the concept of Marit S. Haugen, 1990, Norway. I will use the terms women farmers and professional female farmers in a synonymous way.
2. This research is restricted to the former Federal Republic of Germany.
3. All quotations are my personal translations.
4. This is a code for the identity of the interviewee and location of the quotation in the transcript.

References

Agöl (Arbeitsgem. Ökologischer Landbau e. V.) (1993) Jahresbericht 1992, Darmstadt.

Agrarbericht der Bundesregierung für die Jahre 1987, 1992, 1993, Bonn.

Agrarbündnis e. V. (Hg.) (1993) Landwirtschaft 1993. *Der kritische Agrarbericht. Daten, Berichte, Hintergründe.* Positionen zur Agrardebatte, Bonn.

Aid (Auswertungs- und Informationsdienst für Ernährung, Landwirtschaft und Forsten ev. V.) (1990) *Landbau – alternativ und konventionell*, Bonn.

Beck-Oberdorf, M. (1987) Streitgespräch 'Ökologik gegen Emanzipationslogik'. In *Die Frünen im Bundestag*, AK Frauenpolitik (Hg.) *Frauen und Ökologie. Wider den Machbarkeitswahn*, Köln: S. 122–52.

Bennholdt-Thomsen, V. (1987) Die Ökologiefrage ist eine Frauenfrage. Zum Zusammenhang von Umweltzerstörung, Kapitalakkumulation und Frauenverachtung. In Die Grünen im Bundestag, AK Frauenpolitik (Hg.) *Frauen und Ökologie. Wider den Machbarkeitswahn*, Köln: S. 29–38.

Bennholdt-Thomsen, V. (1989) Die 'Würde der Frau' ist kein Überbauphänomen. Zum Zusammenhang von Geschlecht, Natur und Geld. In *Beiträge zur feministischen Theorie und Praxis,* 12, 24: S. 119–32.

Bioland (Hg.) (1989) Frauen im ökologischen Landbau. In *Bioland,* 16, 6.

Brandth, B. and Bolsø, A. (1991) 'New' women farmers and their use of technology. Paper to the conference *Rural European Women on New Paths,* September 1991, Essen, Germany.

Dabbert, S. and Braun, J. (1993) Auswirkungen des EG-Extensivierungsprogramms auf die Umstellung auf ökologischen Landbau in Baden-Württemberg. In *Agrarwirtschaft,* 42, 2: S. 90–9.

Die Grünen im Bundestag, AK Frauenpolitik (Hg.) (1987) *Frauen und Okologie. Wider den Machbarkeitswahn.* Dokumentation zum Kongreß vom 3–5.10.86, Köln, Kölner Volksblattrerlag.

Glaeser, B. and Strauss, A. (1967) *The Discovery of Grounded Theory.* Chicago, Aldine.

Haugen, M.S. (1990) *The New Generation of Women in Norwegian Agriculture.* Rural Research Paper No. 4, Trondheim.

Hickel, E. (1987) Entstellt männliches Denken die Naturwissenschaft? Kritik und Gegenentwurf aus der Sicht der Frauenforschung. In Die Grünen in Bundestag, AK Frauenpolitik (Hg.) *Frauen und Ökologie. Wider den Machbarkeitswahn.* Köln: S. 100–12.

Jansen, S. (1984) Magie und Technik. Auf der Suche nach feministischen Alternativen zur patriarchalen Naturnutzung. In *Beiträge zur feministischen Theorie und Praxis,* 7, 12: S. 69–81.

Kelly, P.K. (1987) Frauen und Gewaltfreier Widerstand. Oder Anleitungen zum Sturz des internationalen Patriarchats. In Die Grünen im Bundestag, AK Frauenpolitik (Hg.) *Frauen und Okologie. Wider den Machbarkeitswahn.* Köln: S. 19–28.

Lampkin, N. (1993) Okologischer Landbau in Europa. In *Okologie und Landbau,* 21, 86: S. 11–15.

Lauter (1992) Personal information. Landwirtschaftsschule, Grevenbroich.

Lenz, I. (1987) Subsistenzproduktion, Moderne und Freiheit. In Die Grünen im Bundestag, AK Frauenpolitik (Hg.) *Frauen und ökologie. Wider den Machbarkeitswahn.* Köln: S. 71–4.

Lenz, I. (1988) Liebe, Brot und Freiheit: zur neueren Diskussion um Subsistenzproduktion, Technik und Emanzipation in der Frauenforschung. In *Beiträge zur feministischen Theorie und Praxis,* 11, 21/22: S. 167–81.

Mies, M. (1987a) Konturen einer öko-feministischen Gesellschaft. Versuch eines Entwurfs. In Die Grünen im Bundestag, AK Frauenpolitik (Hg.) *Frauen und ökologie. Wider den Machbarkeitswahn.* Köln: S. 39–53.

Mies, M. (1987b) Konturen einer ökofeministischen Gesellschaft. In *Taz* (Die Tageszeitung) vom 26.9.87: S. 8–9.

Mies, M. (1988) Patriarchat und Kapital. *Frauen in der internationalen Arbeitsteilung.* Zürich Rotpunktverlag.

Riechel, J. (1983) Zur Situation von weiblichen Auszubildenden in den Agrarberufen Landwirt/Landwirtin, Winzer/Winzerin und Tierwirt/Tierwirtin. Diplomarbeit, Universität Stuttgart-Hohenheim.

Scheich, E. (1987) Männliche Wissenschaft – Weibliche Ohnmacht? Perspektiven einer feministischen Kritik an Naturwissenschaft und Technik.

In Die Grünen im Bundestag, AK Frauenpolitik (Hg.) *Frauen und Okologie. Wider den Machbarkeitswahn.* Köln: S. 87–99.
Scheich, E. (1989) 'Größer als alle Fenster'. Zur Kritik des Geschlechterverhältnisses und der Naturwissenschaften. In Scheich, E. and Schultz, I. (Hg.) *Soziale Okologie und Feminismus.* Frankfurt/Main, Sozial-ökologische Arbeitspapiere.
Strauss, A. and Corbin, J. (1990) *Basics of Qualitative Research. Grounded Theory Procedures and Techniques.* Newbury Park, Sage Publications.
Werlhof, C.V., Mies, M. and Bennholdt-Thomsen, V. (1983) *Frauen, die letzte Kolonie.* Reinbek bei Hamburg, rororo aktuell.

CHAPTER 7

Rural Women's Environmental Activism in the USA

Carolyn Sachs

Women are key actors in resisting environmental degradation at the grass-roots level. In rural areas, the politics of environmentalism has been extremely controversial. Rural people, especially those who depend on natural resource extraction for their livelihoods, often view environmentalists as outsiders and adversaries. Employment in mining, logging and farming has declined with the concentration of capital and the replacement of labour-intensive work with capital-intensive production techniques. Reliance on resource extraction has become more tenuous in rural areas, although extractive industries continue to dominate in particular local economies. Environmental concerns are often viewed as a further threat to already shrinking job markets in logging and mining. In agriculture, farmers often view environmental concerns as placing further burdens on their already stressed economic situations. As international and national environmental organisations have achieved success and influence in the political arena, people relying on farming, logging or employment in waste-producing industries have feared that their jobs will be threatened. Despite the prevalence of the environment–employment discourse, many people in rural communities are concerned with environmental problems resulting from clearcutting, strip mining, pesticide use in agriculture and the location of toxic waste facilities in rural areas. Numerous grass-roots organisations have formed in rural areas to tackle these and other environmental problems. Due to their particular relations with the environment, women have been particularly active in these environmental groups and have often spurred rural communities to resist environmental damage. Women's importance in grass-roots environmental organisations raises several questions: what is rural women's relationship with the environment? do rural women have a particular stake in ending environmental deterioration? and what are rural women's strategies of resistance? In answer to these questions, this chapter will explore women's activism in three prominent environmental issues in rural areas: sustainable agriculture, forest conservation and toxic wastes.

Women's connections to the environment – ecofeminism/feminist environmentalism

The connections between women and the environment have been brought to light by ecofeminist writers and activists. Ecofeminism, a new social movement that emerged in the 1980s as an outgrowth of the environmental and women's movements, theorises the connections between women and nature. During the 1980s, feminists within the environmental movement became increasingly concerned with the lack of attention to women's issues and began to recognise, problematise and prioritise the connection between the domination of women and the domination of nature (Salleh, 1984; King, 1990). The line of argument put forth by King (1990) suggests that Western patriarchal society has viewed women as closer to nature than men. This connection derives from that culture's dualistic epistemologies which separate nature/culture, mind/body and male/female; associate women with nature and body and men with culture and mind; and finally view males as above nature, body and women. Consequently, the subjugation of women and nature is legitimised. As an outcome of their subordination, women have a stake in ending and challenging the domination of both nature and women and recognise that solutions to ecological problems must be tied to social and gender transformations.

What has emerged under the rubric of ecofeminism is a diverse social movement that encompasses perspectives from socialist feminism, green politics, to a goddess-based spirituality. These wide-ranging perspectives have subjected ecofeminism to critiques from feminists and ecologists alike. Janet Biehl (1991) has written a scathing critique of ecofeminism for rejecting rationalism, essentialising women and moving in non-progressive directions. Bina Agarwal's (1992) less inflammatory and more englightening critique of ecofeminism focuses on the failure of ecofeminism to move beyond the symbolic and ideological associations between women and nature. She suggests that women's and men's relations with the environment must be understood as rooted in their material realities. Using the example of rural Indian women, she suggests that women are both victims of the destruction of nature and also, as a consequence of their daily lives, harbour specific knowledge about the environment. Unlike Biehl (1991), she does not reject the connection between women and environment, but argues that based on their material realities, women have different perspectives on the environment that may provide alternative visions for our relations with the natural world.

The notion that women may provide alternative perspectives and strategies for dealing with environmental problems is consistent with recent scholarship on feminist epistemologies. Feminist standpoint theorists have insisted that women have different ways of knowing and acting based on their common oppression and that this oppression provides them with privileged vantage points for viewing and changing social relations (Harding, 1986). Recent work by Donna Haraway rejects the existence of any one privileged feminist standpoint, but rather calls for:

> politics and epistemologies of location, positioning and situating, where partiality and not universality is the condition of being heard to make rational knowledge claims. These are claims on people's lives; the view from a body, always a complex, contradictory, structuring and structured body, versus the view from above, from nowhere, from simplicity. (1991: 195)

Thus, Haraway argues for a politics of location and insists that all knowledge claims are partial and situated. Haraway's call for valuing 'situated knowledge' is congruent with Agarwal's insistence that rural women's particular connections to the environment must be understood as connected to their daily lives in specific localities.

Agarwal (1992) poses the term 'feminist environmentalism' as an alternative to ecofeminism in an attempt to move beyond the symbolic connections between women and nature with the goal of struggling with resources as well as meanings. Feminist environmentalism would operate on both feminist and environmental fronts.

> On the feminist front there would be a need to challenge and transform both notions about gender and the actual division of work and resources between the genders. On the environmental front there would be a need to challenge and transform not only notions about the relationship between people and nature but also the actual methods of appropriation of nature's resources by a few. (Agarwal, 1992: 127)

Agarwal (1992) proceeds to discuss rural Indian women's lives from the perspective of feminist environmentalism. Here, I will attempt to explore US rural women's activism related to the environment from the standpoint of feminist environmentalism.

Gender and the rural environment

Rural women have particular standpoints based on the gender division of labour in rural areas and the particular forms that sexual domination assumes in such areas. Rural women do not have a singular standpoint, but their knowledge is situated in their localities and daily activities. The gendered nature of daily activities in most rural areas in the USA offers the possibility of seeing differently. While rural women's standpoints are preferred because they are 'subjugated', they remain partial. Rural women's subjugated and situated knowledge offers possibilities for a different, and possibly emancipatory, knowledge and social action, but these possibilities are weakly articulated, exemplifying the problem of how to see from below (Haraway, 1991). Rural women's knowledge and experience has only rarely been transformed into feminist politics and activism. Due to the particular patriarchal relations that characterise social relations in rural areas, rural women have resisted, but only rarely directly challenged, patriarchal dominance. Few voices have suggested that feminist theorists can provide key insights into environmental changes in agriculture. A recent exception is an intriguing article by Kloppenburg (1991) who suggests that feminist epistemologies, especially Haraway's notion of partial perspectives, proves useful in establishing conversations that might change the trajectory of agriculture and agricultural science.

In order to understand rural women's environmental activism, it is useful to explore three aspects of gender relations in rural areas that set the stage for women's particular relations with the environment and their efforts to tackle environmental problems. Firstly, access to the environment is gendered. In rural areas, land is the most basic resource and women's legal access to land is limited; men own and control the vast majority of land in the United States. Data for total land ownership are difficult to obtain, but in terms of farmland, women are sole owners of 4 per cent of US farmland (USDA, 1987). Of course, rural women often have access to land through joint ownership with their husbands or through use rights granted by their families. Whatmore's (1991) insightful study of women on family farms in England emphasises the importance of land for farming and women's exclusion from ownership. Land is extremely significant in the social relation of farming as well as the resource that provides access to credit and therefore other forms of capital. On English farms, land is the principal asset and provides a high collateral base for borrowing. Like English farm women, women on farms in the USA have historically been denied access to land and therefore to the principal assets in farming. Therefore, their relations to land and their power in terms of decision-making on agricultural land must usually be negotiated through other family members.

In the USA large tracts of land are publicly owned and therefore legally accessible to all people. However, much public land is used for mining, timber, energy extraction and military purposes, thus limiting public access to this land. Other land is maintained for natural areas, wilderness and wildlife. Women, as well as men, have access to this land, but this space is often dominated by men and used for male-centred recreational activities such as hunting and fishing. Although women are not legally prevented from using these public spaces, they are often uncomfortable, cautious or afraid to enter wilderness areas.

Secondly, economic activities related to the environment are gendered. Local rural areas that have been primarily dependent on extractive industries such as mining and timber are changing and pose particular sets of problems and opportunities for rural women. Regions dependent on mining and logging have been characterised by boom and bust cycles, high levels of poverty and extreme sex segregation of jobs. Miners and loggers are overwhelmingly men. Women have largely been excluded from extractive or 'dangerous' work based on biological arguments emphasising women's limited physical strength or the need to protect women from hazardous work. For example, women's exclusion from coal mining was nearly complete until 1973 when federal legislation forced mine operators to hire women; nevertheless, their gains have been minimal (Tallichet, 1991).

Land and resources are typically owned by outside corporate interests resulting in minimal local control and marginal local benefits. In both the mining and timber industries, capital has been increasingly substituted for labour, often with severe environmental consequences. Strip-mining and clear cutting do extreme damage to the environment and rely on large-scale machinery and less labour than other types of mining and logging operations. During the boom periods, men are often employed in high-wage unionised jobs, however, there are often interspersed periods of unemployment as well as high injury rates. Women in these areas have few opportunities for economic independence, have often depended on male wages for income, have been active in defending men's rights to jobs and are particularly vulnerable to slipping in and out of poverty (Maggard, 1990).

Women are more likely to work in agriculture than in forests or mines. The social organisation of farms as family enterprises has meant that women have been extensively involved in farming. Fifty-four per cent of farm women consider themselves to be main operators of their farms, with most of these women involved in partnerships with their husbands, sons or other family members. Women work on farms but gender divisions of tasks and responsibilities as well as patriarchal traditions often result in men controlling land, capital and management on farms (Rosenfeld, 1985). There are exceptions; approximately 12 per cent of US farmers are women. Patriarchal organisation of farms has set the stage for women's continuing lack of access to capital to enter farming (Whatmore, 1991). Also, with the decline in family farms and increasing prominence of large-scale agricultural operations, women are hired extensively to work in specific labour-intensive tasks such as harvesting vegetable crops or working in poultry houses. The proportion of women hired workers in agriculture has increased substantially in the USA in the past several decades. Despite women's extensive work in agriculture, men continue to control and dominate agricultural production. Thus, rural women are less likely than men to have control over property, management and decisions in farming, logging and mining, those industries involved in resource extraction. Many women's livelihoods are linked to natural resource extraction either through their own participation in these industries or as a result of their economic dependency on men who are employed in such occupations.

Thirdly, women's responsibility for reproductive labour such as daily physical care of adults, children and infants; maintaining social relations, giving birth and caring for the sick, often ties them more closely to human health concerns. As recent breakthroughs in feminist epistemology suggest, women have particular perspectives and situated knowledge based on their everyday life experiences. Within the socialist feminist tradition various scholars such as Rose, Hartsock and Smith have different conceptions concerning what exactly are the everyday life experiences that inform women's different standpoints. Hilary Rose (1983) emphasises that the unity of hand, brain and heart that characterises women's work provides women with a different and fuller basis of knowing in contrast to men's activities which typically separate mental and manual labour and often do not include emotional labour. For Hartsock (1983), women's immersion in subsistence and childcare activities places them in a world that is more sensuous, concrete and relational than the world men typically inhabit. Dorothy Smith (1987), a sociologist who has long advocated the existence of a feminist standpoint, also sees women's standpoint as deriving from their work activities. Because women take care of men's bodies and the local places where they exist, men are free to dwell in the world of the abstract. The particular character of women's activities also enables men to inhabit a different world and to interpret the world in a distorted fashion. In terms of attention to environmental and health concerns, men's typical daily lives are not embedded in care of local people and places. Smith contends that the more successfully women perform their work the more invisible it becomes to men – thus women's work is constructed socially as natural, instinctual or emotional. Here, I would like to suggest that women's responsibility for caring labour provides them with vantage points or particular situated knowledge such that they are often the first to suspect or detect environmental problems, especially as it affects human health. This is not to suggest that women are biologically closer to nature than men or to essentialise women's caring activities, rather as Agarwal (1992) suggests, the particular gender division of labour, in this case, women's responsibility for reproductive labour, ties them more closely to human health concerns.

Also, increasing epidemiological evidence suggests that women's bodies are frequently the earliest markers of environmental damage in the form of miscarriages, breast cancer and cervical cancer. For many women, health concerns for their families and communities have been the initial motivating factor for their environmental activism. German feminists have critiqued the transfer of responsibility for health to women and unsuccessfully called on women to resist the call to minimise waste that increases women's work and erroneously places responsibility for waste and health on women (Schultz, 1993). Despite these calls, Schultz notes that women remain concerned about waste due to their feelings of responsibility for the health of their children, their husbands and for their own health. They have protested against construction of waste incinerator plants due to their fear of cancer and become engaged in social movements because they take care of, and comfort, people who become chronically ill.

Rural women's resistance

Having discussed three aspects of gender relations that affect women's environmental activism in rural areas, it is also important to note how environmental activism is related to other social movements and how the particular forms of rural women's environmental activism are related to the gendered nature of political activities and strategies of resistance.

Women's resistance to environmental problems can be understood in the context of the broader social movements that have proliferated since the mid-

1970s in the USA and elsewhere. Social movements emphasising peace, feminism, ecology, local autonomy, race, ethnicity and sexuality have gained ascendance at the same time that workplace organising has decreased in effectiveness. Political theorists, especially more orthodox Marxists, question-ed the progressive potential of these new social movements and emphasised that true progressive political action occurred at the level of production in the workplace with unions serving as the principal site for democratic action (Krauss, 1987). Community politics or identity politics were viewed as misdirected or futile forms of protest that held little hope for social change. However, the persistence and strength of these social movements have signalled a reinterpretation of their potential among Marxists and other political theorists. Protest is increasingly occurring to preserve or improve the structures of everyday life, rather than at the level of production (Cohen, 1985). Thus, feminist, environmental, racial and sexuality movements have clearly moved into the mainstream of resistance politics. Also, there has been increasing recognition that issues of these various social movements are connected. The environmental movement has been challenged by feminists and racial and ethnic minorities for failing to see the links between oppression of women and people of colour and environment destruction. Two new perspec-tives within the environmental movement that link social concerns with environmental issues are ecofeminism and environmental justice.

Understanding women's strategies of resistance involves redefining what counts as resistance (Aptheker, 1989). Rather than seeing women as helpless victims of an all powerful patriarchal ideology who are unable to resist, there is a need to account for women's potential for creativity and agency within a context of limited options. Social structures are not only constraining but are also enabling, thus they are not simply barriers to action but also preconditions for the possibility of meaningful choices (Felski, 1989).

For many women opportunities for resistance are shaped by the dailiness of their lives; resistance is more than organised struggle. Aptheker's (1989) book, *Tapestries of Life,* captivatingly illustrates the importance of looking beyond organised struggles to the daily lives of women for their acts of resistance. For example, for many African-American women, the constraints for racism, sexism and poverty have made it difficult to participate in organised political action; however, these black women have clearly struggled against multiple oppressions (Collins, 1990). Women fight back using a wide range of verbal and interactional strategies (Stanley, 1990). For rural women, patriarchal forms and traditional values have prevailed and organised feminist struggles have been relatively rare. Rather, women's resistance strategies have taken a variety of forms. Traditional understandings of resistance as social rather than individual, political rather than personal, and inclusive of large numbers of people in conscious alliance working towards a common goal, often misinter-prets women's activities as outside of politics.

Others have argued that redefining resistance necessitates a broader con-ceptualisation of what constitutes the appropriate subject matter of politics (Fraser, 1989). Politics is normally contrasted with economics or personal issues, thereby shielding economic and personal issues from political contestation (Fraser, 1989). Thus it becomes necessary to legitimate women's needs as genuine political issues as opposed to either private, or market, matters. Because women's oppression is often rooted in personal conditions such as family, marriage, sexuality and motherhood, women are contesting the boundaries of what is political. Women's acts of resistance take many forms and have often been unseen or under-appreciated for their cumulative effects. Consequently women's activism, including their environmental activism, is often invisible or not recognised as political resistance. For example, a recent survey of 7,010 people in the USA found that although women express more concern than men about environmental problems, they report lower levels of environmental activism than men (Mothai, 1991). Mothai (1992) finds little explanation for the discrepancy for women's environmental concern and levels of activism in his data. Women's lower level of involvement in political organisations does not explain the differences in environmental activism; the gap between men and women in environmental activity is greater than the gap in general political activity. He suggests some possibilities: women may be involved in local environmental issues, women's participation in other issues involving concerns with social, economic and political equality, or perhaps the measures of environmental activism used in the study should be broadened. The results of his study suggest that typical measures of environmental activism may miss or skim over women's participation. Another recent study of women in the US civil rights movement provides evidence to suggest that women face greater opposition to participation in social movements than their male counterparts (McAdam, 1992). Thus, I suggest that rural women's environmental activism must be defined broadly to include struggles for survival, maintaining the conditions of existence, as well as organised opposition to environmental degradation.

One type of resistance frequently engaged in by women is creating the conditions necessary for life. In situations where these conditions are continuously being undermined, women's struggles for survival and connection with their families should be considered acts of resistance against corporate or government interests that destroy forests, pollute groundwater or spray herbicides on crops. For example, individual women's efforts to rid their surroundings of toxic substances can be considered resistance, not merely a non-political personal, individual or family concern. A second type of rural women's environmental activism is involvement in organisations and groups opposed to environmental destruction. Even in these efforts, women's resistance frequently takes different forms from men's resistance. Women's marginalisation or exclusion from traditional centres of power in rural areas such as trade unions, farm organisations, political parties and environmental organisations has meant they must turn to other forms of resistance (see Chapter 4). Thus, women's involvement in the environmental movement is predominantly at the grass-roots and community level, as they have largely been excluded from decision-making positions in mainstream environmental organisations.

Several common themes emerge in women's activist strategies. Women's acts are often efforts to forge connections such as the creation of networks and community associations. They view themselves as entering public arenas not as isolated individuals but as members of households and communities. Through their daily activities women are often strongly rooted in class, ethnic and cultural communities and work hard at maintaining networks and relationships that give life to communities (Ackelsburg, 1988). Forming connections is not always a progressive act and attempts to preserve communities or cultural heritage may be imbedded within racist, xenophobic, homophobic and patriarchal systems. Many women have internalised the view of their place as subordinates and may be resigned or reactionary in their political positions. Feminism is not widely embraced by rural women. Rural women's involvement in political action is often not with organised feminism and they often reject the label feminist, but this by no means suggests that women do not resist domination. As Aptheker suggests, women's daily activities to preserve the conditions for life for their families must be considered resistance when these conditions are constantly threatened. Women's efforts to protect the environment have been in women's (not necessarily feminist) organisations as well as in male-dominated organisations. Many of the activities of rural women are to forge connections with their families and communities rather than merely to improve their individual situations. Sometimes these activities are individually empowering as well as improving broader conditions for life. Women's activism does not always make them conscious of what they share as women, and at times they are involved in movements that reinforce rather than challenge their place of subordination.

Three key environmental issues in rural areas in which women have been instrumental in grass-roots activities, are sustainable agriculture, forest conservation and toxic/hazardous wastes. Women's experiences in these three movements are documented below based on interviews, studies and reports by rural women concerning their efforts. This methodological strategy is used to describe women's involvement using their own voices.

Women in the sustainable agriculture movement

The sustainable agriculture movement emerged in the late 1970s as a response to environmental problems associated with agricultural production, particularly pesticide use, and the increasing power of agribusiness. Grass-roots organisations of farmers, consumers and environmentalists have pushed issues of pesticide poisonings, organic agriculture, groundwater contamination and concentration of farmland into the forefront of discussions on agriculture and farm policies and programmes. Concern with the environmental impacts of agricultural practices has filtered into national and international debates on farm and food policies to the extent that sustainable agriculture has become a buzzword in mainstream agricultural institutions such as The World Bank, the United States Department of Agriculture and other national and international agencies involved in agriculture. Thus, on the one hand, the sustainable agriculture movement has been remarkably successful in establishing the importance of environmental concerns in agriculture, but on the other, the agenda for sustainable agriculture has simultaneously been narrowed to technical approaches for reducing the environmental impacts of agricultural practices without questioning other problems in agriculture that were raised by initial advocates of sustainability concerning the inequitable class, race and gender relations in agriculture (Allen and Sachs, 1992).

To explore women's position and experience in the sustainable agriculture movement, I conducted in-depth interviews with women farmers, activists and academic leaders in the sustainable agriculture movement in California in 1990. My interviews will be supplemented by Grace Gershuny's (1991) interviews of women and men in the organic agricultural movement and writings of other women activists in sustainable agriculture.

Women are key players in the sustainable agriculture movement at the grassroots level; often taking the lead in organising local chapters, meetings, writing newsletters and organising conferences. Much of the early organising work in establishing a statewide organic agriculture organisation and network was accomplished by women. As one of the state leaders affirmed, 'women are often working behind the scenes. All of my good volunteers that helped organise conferences and do mailings were women. Men have a way of getting into positions that are more glorious.' Or, as a woman from Oregon in the USA explained:

> It's interesting to note that most of the pesticide education work and environmental awareness on the local level is done by women. I've noticed that conferences seem to be attended by a lot of six-foot tall white men, but they're all organised by women. The kind of work that has kept the organisation stable has been done by women. (As quoted in Gershuny, 1991: 8)

Women work as volunteers in local or state sustainable agriculture organisations, but are less likely than men to be in visible leadership positions. Also, as the sustainable agriculture movement becomes increasingly influential and institutionalised, men attain leadership positions. Although men are in leadership positions, there is more room for women's involvement at decision-making levels in sustainable agriculture organisations than in traditional farm organisations.

In addition to their direct involvement in sustainable agriculture organisations, women living on farms attempt to make their farms healthier places to live and work and to produce healthier food. Women organic farmers that I interviewed reported various reasons for their commitment to organic farming: concern with the toxic effects of pesticides, taking care of land, interest in ecology and problems with the organisation of the food system. Several women explained that they had become involved with organic agriculture when it was quite marginal and expressed that the mainstreaming of organic agriculture has been a mixed blessing. Women organic farmers expressed concern that 'large producers will squeeze out little people who are doing organic production because they believe in it' and that 'bigger farmers want to put their land into organic production to make a profit, but for me it is a commitment'.

Although there was no consensus among the women I interviewed concerning the existence of a unique women's perspective to farming, many of them reported that they did approach farming differently from their husbands, but also recognised that there were differences between women and refuted an essentialist position. One woman explained the difference between women and men on organic farms:

> My women friends know it's crazy to get on the production treadmill – we don't want our lives to be like that and want to hold on to family and social values as well as producing more. There is a tendency for male egos (and women with these egos) to get caught up in the money cycle and lose sight of why we are farming organically. This emphasis on production makes our lives insane and we need to think about slowing down a bit.

Grace Gershuny asked the women and men she interviewed 'Have women served as the guardians of organic values, and can organic values be considered to be feminine values? How does this relate to feminism and to men in organic agriculture?' (1991: 10). Some women responded that women do have a unique approach because of their experience as mothers, although they insisted that these experiences were cultural rather than biological. Several of the women questioned whether there is such a thing as 'feminine values' and noted that men in the organic agriculture movement tend to share caring and environmental values.

Dana Jackson, a co-founder of the Land Institute, suggests that aspects of women's culture can be combined with approaches to ecology to transform agriculture. The Land Institute is an organisation that has led the way in developing a vision for the long-term sustainability of agriculture through promoting ecological approaches to agriculture. Research at the Land Institute has focused on

> creating a partnership with nature in which elements of the ecosystem contribute to soil fertility and insect and disease control. Our focus on bringing ecology and agriculture together naturally embraces some of the qualities of women's culture . . . . For example, our researchers must pay close attention to the growth habits of particular needs of each species and their pest species. We must think about how our crops will relate to each other and the places where they grow. Nurturing the plants where they are, rather than conquering the environment where we want them to grow, will be our emphasis. (Jackson, 1992: 37)

Women's efforts have been central to the success of the sustainable agriculture movement, however, feminist concerns have rarely emerged as key issues. As the sustainable agriculture movement becomes institutionalised, men have emerged as leaders and eclipsed women's grass-roots activities. It seems that at this juncture, when women's knowledge and activities are discredited in favour of scientific research and bureaucratic control, that women's voices will call for attention to deeper ecological and social questions.

Forest conservation

Problems associated with the destruction of the world's forests have gained world-wide attention in the 1990s. Multinational corporations, financial institutions and national governments are depleting the world's remaining forests to attain timber and in some instances to expand agriculture. The environmental movement has emphasised the deep dependence of humans on the forest for their prosperity in connection with biological diversity, global climate stability, and soil and water conservation. Rural people, especially indigenous people, have long recognised the connections between their lives and the existence of the forest. However, the US government has often sided with timber interests in managing forests primarily as timber resources to be harvested. Rural people living in forested areas of the USA have relied on jobs in the lumber industry as a primary source of employment.

Protection of land and wildlife areas in North America has been a long-standing concern of many environmental organisations. Conservation organisations such as the Sierra Club and National Audubon Society, founded in the late 1800s and early 1900s, were concerned with species preservation and preservation of particular locations. By the late 1960s the conservation movement adopted a more ecological approach, based partially on Rachel Carson's exposition of problems related to DDT, and an awareness that environmental problems were not necessarily site-specific and adopted strategies broader than conserving particular areas of wilderness (Dunlap and Mertig, 1992). In addition to these mainstream and influential environmental groups that have been involved in forest conservation efforts, there are numerous other organisations working to save forests.

Women have been involved in various strategies to save the forests in the western USA ranging from participation in radical environmental groups such as Earth First!'s efforts to prevent logging of redwood forests to working with local organisations to fight toxics in forests.

In northern California, Kathy Hall led a local organisation that is concerned with the effects of the US Forest Service practices of spraying herbicides for vegetation control. As she describes:

> I come from Stewart Springs, a small town nestled in a narrow valley lining a rugged ridge of mountains called The Eddies in northern California. My life is intimately connected to these mountains and the people who live there. Most of the land is public, managed by the US Forest Service, or mismanaged as the local say. The Forest Service views toxic herbicides as the most cost-effective method for killing off unwanted forest vegetation and improving the productivity of the conifers. The most common herbicides used were 22, 4–D and 2, 4, 5–T, defoliants used by the US military to deforest Vietnam. (Hall, as quoted in Light, 1992: 15)

As the health effects of these practices began to appear, Kathy Hall recounts, 'people began to experience unusual health problems. Particularly alarming were the high rates of spontaneous miscarriages, the rare moll pregnancy, children born with cleft palates, hearing problems, and low birth rates' (as quoted in Light, 1992: 15). Kathy Hall explains that she 'couldn't just sit idly by watching the forests and people being poisoned. So I threw myself into organising, gathering information, and politicking' (Light, 1992: 15). She led a local group to protest the health effects of government spraying, conducted research on problems, collected reports from individuals and agencies, spoke at meetings and testified at public hearings. This intense level of activity came at a high personal cost and resulted in a broken marriage. Her husband complained about a dirty house, expensive phone bills and her attendance at too many meetings. The conflict between political involvement and personal life is echoed by many women environmental activists.

Not all women living in forested regions of the USA are friends of the environmental movement. In the Pacific Northwest, where local battles have taken shape between those advocating environmental protection and those fighting for the maintenance of timber-related jobs, women are on both sides of the issue. Both men and women have been involved in radical regional organisations such as Earth First! that attempts to protect the redwoods in northern California. The level of anti-environmentalist sentiments is illustrated by a 1990 incident in which a pipe bomb exploded in a car carrying two Earth First! activists, Judi Bari and Darryl Cherney who were organising 'Redwood Summer' to protest clear-cutting in ancient California forests (Devall, 1992). Wives of timber workers have joined their husbands to protest against environmentalists and environmental legislation in northern California. A speech by a former member of the California Board of Forestry to the Redwood Region Logging Conference in 1991 called for a People First! movement to counter the Earth First! environmental movement. His blindness to women's participation on both sides of the issue is apparent in his rather macho challenge to the group, 'I'm betting that there are some of you out there who are tired of turning the other cheek and are ready to kick somebody in the crotch' (Devall, 1992: 60).

Another example of women's support of logging is a community in Oregon where environmental groups were successful in halting logging to protect the spotted owl. Women married to loggers in the local community led efforts to oppose environmentalists' attempts to protect the forest. These women are dependent on their husbands' incomes from logging for economic support. Although they see the forest as important to their economic well-being, they do not directly depend on the forest to supply their daily sustenance. In this case, women married to loggers support their husbands' right to earn income even if it means destruction of the forest. These women define their interests as the same as those of their husbands and are not likely to be supportive of resistance efforts organised by non-local people to protect their local forests.

Toxic waste

Individual women's efforts such as Lois Gibbs' fight at Love Canal have come to symbolise women's resistance to environmental pollution in their homes and neighbourhoods. Freudenberg and Steinsapir (1992) describe grass-roots environmentalism in the USA as a loosely structured movement consisting of community-based groups, regional or state coalitions, and national organisations with estimates of 1,300 to 7,000 grass-roots environmental groups. These groups are usually started by local people in response to problems such as toxic dumps, pesticide spraying, air pollution, contaminated water supplies, radioactive wastes, nuclear plants and location of incinerators and hazardous waste disposal facilities (Freudenberg and Steinsapir, 1992). Women are heavily represented in local organisations. Increased environmental awareness and success of grass-roots community organising have resulted in efforts by manufacturers of toxic wastes to locate their plants and disposal sites in remote rural areas to avoid regulations and political resistance. The coincidence between location of toxic wastes and presence of high percentage minority populations is extremely high in the USA (Commission for Racial Justice, 1987). Hazardous waste sites are increasingly located in regions populated by high proportions of Native Americans, African-Americans and Latinos. Urban ghettos and rural blackbelt communities are often targeted as sites for hazardous waste landfills and incinerators. Three of the nation's largest commercial hazardous waste sites were located in African-American or Latino communities in 1987, accounting for 40 per cent of US hazardous waste disposal capacity (Commission for Racial Justice, 1987). Rural people are increasingly mobilising to fight location of waste facilities in their communities. Small groups of people, the majority of whom are often women, are fighting health hazards in their communities. Thus, rural women, especially women of colour, have been instrumental in fighting placement of hazardous and toxic wastes in their communities. A growing number of African-American grass-roots environmental groups are being formed that simultaneously confront equity and environmental issues (Bullard and Wright, 1992).

Several examples of rural women who have been active in fighting toxic and hazardous waste in their communities exemplify the efforts and problems faced by rural women activists. Lisa Crawford began to organise her community in rural Ohio when she discovered that her well was contaminated by a nearby plant (Crawford, 1992). Upon discovery that the plant that was adorned with red and white checks displaying a sign that read 'Feeding and Maintenance Center' was not a Purina Dog Food factory, but a nuclear weapons facility operated by the federal government, Lisa Crawford began investigating the health impact of nuclear waste from the site. In her town, she spearheaded an organisation that was comprised largely of women. Through many battles with the Pentagon, scientists, unions and in the courts, and accusations of being hysterical and in need of psychiatric help, their organisation successfully closed the facility and continues to work with issues of site cleanup.

Another rural woman has led the fight against production and location of toxic nuclear wastes on federal land in Oklahoma. Jesse DeerInWater, a Native American woman, is fighting the location of nuclear production facilities in her largely Native American community. She describes her initial efforts upon learning that a uranium conversion facility was to be located in her community:

I knew that I had to organise, so I started talking to people. About 20 per cent of the people in our areas are Native American, mostly Cherokee, and I started with them because I thought, on some level, we had some kind of treaty rights. Also, I knew we were at an advantage being Native Americans. We didn't have to overcome any brainwashing about the government working for our best interests. I heard a lot of 'You're crazy, Jessie, they've already killed Karen Silkwood'. (DeerInWater, 1992: 15)

Presently she is involved in an effort to halt testing of nuclear wastes as fertilizer near her hometown and has attempted to challenge findings by an agronomist at Oklahoma State University who insists there are no health problems associated with grazing cows on land treated with nuclear waste.

Both of these women's efforts to protect the health of their families and communities have led them to become involved in broader political issues. Jesse DeerInWater has been instrumental in starting an organisation of indigenous people to protect the environment. In her attempt to develop strategies to close the nuclear weapons facility near her home, Lisa Crawford was referred to Jesse DeerInWater for advice. Critics of these groups have noted the 'not in my backyard' mentality. But once these connections were made, Lisa realised closing the plant and relocating the waste to land where Native Americans lived was not sufficient. Currently she is involved in litigation to force the federal government not simply to move the waste from her community, but to prove that safe storage facilities are available and ensure that other communities are not the new victims. A shift from a concern with local community pollution and health problems, a philosophy of 'not in my backyard', to a philosophy of 'not in anybody's backyard' has become characteristic of the toxics movement (Freudenberg and Steinsapir, 1992). Neither of these women considered themselves feminists or environmental activists when they began their activities to halt hazardous waste production and disposal in their communities, but as they proceeded they began to understand broader political implications of their work and the particular implications for women.

Women activists who battle toxic waste issues have often been dismissed, denigrated and referred to as 'hysterical housewives' by legislators, government officials and policy-makers. Cora Tucker, an activist in Virginia, details her experience with the label hysterical housewife. She describes that when she was first in groups of women at the Virginia legislature where women were labelled as hysterical housewives she used to become upset and cry as she thought of herself as merely a hysterical housewife. Now she explains 'I've learned that's a tactic men use to keep us in our place' and her approach to the charge has switched.

When I started the stuff of toxic waste and nuclear waste, I went back to the General Assembly and a guy gets up and says, 'We have a whole room full of hysterical housewives today, so men we need to get prepared.' I said, 'you're exactly right. We're hysterical and when it comes to matters of life and death, especially mine, I get hysterical.' And

I said, 'If men don't get hysterical, there's something wrong with them.'
(As quoted in Light, 1992: 14)

Conclusion

Connections between rural women and the environment in the USA set the
stage for women's involvement in environmental issues. Work by ecofeminists
led the way in pointing out connections between the domination of women and
nature and suggesting possibilities for transforming relations of domination.
However, much of the earlier work of ecofeminists focused primarily on
symbolic connections between women and nature and glossed over women's
actual situated knowledge and local experiences. Bina Agarwal's call for a
feminist environmentalism, that encompasses insights from ecofeminism
within a material and political economic perspective provides a more convincing perspective for understanding rural women's relations with the environment. Agarwal's recognition for the need of feminist environmentalism is
accompanied by the recognition that forms of resistance are gendered and
must be viewed broadly. Women's resistance to environmental deterioration
comes in their struggles to improve the daily living conditions of their families
and neighbourhoods as well as in their organised participation in grass-roots
and mainstream environmental groups.

In exploring rural women's involvement in sustainable agriculture, forest
conservation and hazardous waste movements, three broad conclusions
emerge. Firstly, rural women, because of the nature of their daily activities, are
often the first to recognise and organise around local environmental issues to
limit the use of toxics in agriculture, conserve forests and fight toxic waste
disposal. Issues of their own health as well as the health of their children,
families and communities has often been at the forefront of women's efforts.
While some feminist theorists have warned that women should not take
responsibility for health or waste issues, the lessons here suggest that women
do take these responsibilities seriously, and that a feminist environmentalist
position is needed where women's voices are heeded as entrenched interests are
undermined (Agarwal, 1992). Secondly, resistance strategies are gendered.
Women lack access to formal power structures, rarely emerging as leaders in
mainstream environmental organisations, but often providing the bulk of effort
in local organisations. Thus, in rural areas, women have been instrumental in
forming grass-roots organisations to tackle local problems. In many instances,
their work in particular localities has led them to link with groups in other
regions.

Thirdly, rural women do not necessarily support environmental issues.
Many of the environmental battles in rural areas are translated into a struggle
between jobs versus the environment. In such efforts, men's jobs are often
threatened. Women who personally have a stake in resource extraction or
whose husbands' jobs are threatened may well be opposed to environmental
activities. This finding lends credence to Haraway's claim that there is no one
women's standpoint or perspective, but rather women's perspectives and ways

of interpreting the world are grounded in their local and situated knowledge. Fourthly, there is variation in the extent that feminist and broader social issues come to the fore in environmental discourse and actions. Many of the women involved in environmental activism do not consider themselves feminists, but there is a growing recognition that women are doing the groundbreaking work. These women often become empowered through their organisational work as they begin to make links with other women. For many of these women, involvement in environmental groups has transformed their lives, their ways of interpreting the world, and their political understandings. Often the transformations are personally painful – as they have endured divorce, isolation by their neighbours, questioning of their sanity, as well as struggles with governments, corporations and environmental organisations. Their work has often been appropriated by men, who take the stage as political, scientific or administrative leaders of environmental movements and organisations, and often leave behind broader social agendas. But increasingly within the environmental movement, there is a growing recognition that social justice issues are connected to environmental problems.

Feminist environmentalism faces many challenges, but may well provide ways of thinking and acting that can transform gender relations and relations between humans and the non-human world through seriously questioning the distribution of property, economic privilege, power and knowledge.

References

Agarwal, B. (1992) The gender and environment debate: lessons from India. *Feminist Studies,* 18(a): 119–58.

Allen, P. and Sachs, C. (1992) The social side of sustainability: class, gender and race. *Science as Culture,* 2(13): 569–90.

Amott, T. and Mothai, J. (1990) *Race, Gender, and Work.* Boston, South End Press.

Aptheker, B. (1989) *Tapestries of Life: Women's Consciousness and the Meaning of Daily Experience.* Amherst, University of Massachusetts Press.

Biehl, J. (1991) *Rethinking Ecofeminist Politics.* Boston, South End Press.

Bullard, R. and Wright, B. (1992) The quest for environmental equity: mobilizing the African-American community for social change: 39–40. In Dunlap, R. and Mertig, A. (eds) *American Environmentalism: The U.S. Environmental Movement, 1970–1990.* Philadelphia, Taylor and Francis.

Cohen, J.L. (1985) Strategy of identity: new theoretical paradigms and contemporary social movements. *Social Research,* 52(4): 663–716.

Collins, P.H. (1990) *Black Feminist Thought: Knowledge, Consciousness, and the Politics of Empowerment.* Boston, Unwin Hyman.

Commission for Racial Justice (1987) *Toxic Wastes and Race: A National Report on the Racial and Socioeconomic Characteristics of Communities with Hazardous Wastes Sites.* New York, United Church of Christ.

Crawford, L. (1992) Military facilities pollution in the American Midwest. Paper presented at Engendering Environmental Thinking Conference. Cambridge, MA, Massachusetts Institute of Technology, 20–22 May.

134

DeerInWater, J. (1992) The war against nuclear waste disposal. *Sojourner,* 17(11): 15.

Devall, B. (1992) Deep ecology and radical environmentalism: 51–62. In Dunlap, R. and Mertig, A. (eds) *American Environmentalism: The US Environmental Movement 1970–1990.* Philadelphia, Taylor and Francis.

Dunlap, R. and Mertig, A. (1992) The evolution of the U.S. environmental movement from 1970 to 1990: and overview: 1–10. In Dunlap, R. and Mertig, A. (eds) In *American Environmentalism: The U.S. Environmental Movement, 1970–1990.* Philadelphia, Taylor and Francis.

Felski, R. (1989) Feminist theory and social change. *Theory, Culture and Society,* 6: 219–40.

Fraser, N. (1989) *Unruly Practices: Power, Discourse and Gender in Contemporary Social Theory.* Minneapolis, University of Minnesota Press.

Freudenberg, N. and Steinsapir, C. (1992) Not in our backyards; the grassroots environmental movement; 27–38. In Dunlap, R. and Mertig, A. (eds) *American Environmentalism: The U.S. Environmental Movement, 1970–1990.* Philadelphia, Taylor and Francis.

Gershuny, G. (1991) Women in alternative agriculture. *Organic Farmer,* 2(3): 5–21.

Haraway, D. (1991) *Simians, Cyborgs and Women: The Reinvention of Nature.* New York, Routledge.

Harding, S. (1986) *The Science Question in Feminism.* Ithaca, NY, Cornell University Press.

Hartsock, N. (1983) The feminist standpoint: developing the ground for a specifically feminist historical materialism: 283–310. In Harding, S. and Hintikka, M. (eds) *Discovering Reality: Feminist Perspectives on Opistemology, Metaphysics, Methodology, and Philosophy of Science.* Dordrecht, Reidel.

Jackson, D. (1992) Women and the challenge of the ecological era. *The Ecologist,* 22(1): 32–8.

King, Y. (1990) Healing the wounds: feminism, ecology and the nature/culture dualism: 128–54. In Diamond, I. and Orenstein, G. (eds) *Reweaving the World: the Emergence of Ecofeminism.* San Franciso, Sierra Club Books.

Kloppenburg, J. (1991) Social theory and the de/reconstruction of agricultural science: local knowledge for an alternative agriculture. *Rural Sociology,* 54(4): 519–48.

Krauss, C. (1987) Community struggles and the state. Paper presented at American Sociological Association Meetings, Chicago, August.

Light, A. (1992) Hysterical housewives or committed campaigners? Women activists in North America. *The Ecologist,* 22(1): 14–15.

McAdam, D. 61992) Gender as a mediator of the activist experience: the case of freedom summer. *American Journal of Sociology,* 95(5): 1211–40.

Maggard, S.W. (1990) Gender contested: women's participation in the Brookside Coal Strike 75–98. In West, G. and Blumberg, R. (eds) *Women and Social Protest.* New York, Oxford University Press.

Mothai, P. (1992) Men, women, and the environment: an examination of the gender gap in environmental concern and activism. *Society and Natural Resources,* 5: 1–19.

Rose, H. (1983) Hand, brain, and heart: a feminist epistemology for the natural sciences. *Signs,* 9(1): 73–90.

Rosenfeld, R. (1985) *Farm Women: Work, Farm and Family in the United States.* Chapel Hill, University of North Carolina Press.

Salleh, A. (1984) Deeper than deep ecology: the ecofeminist connection. *Environmental Ethics,* 6: 339–45.

Schultz, I. (1993) Women and waste. *Capitalism, Nature, Socialism,* 4(2): 51–63.

Smith, D. (1987) *The Everyday World as Problematic: A Feminist Sociology.* Boston, Northeastern University Press.

Stanley, L. (1990) *Feminist Praxis.* New York, Routledge.

Tallichet, S. (1991) *Moving Up Down in the Mine: Sex Segregation in Underground Coal Mining.* Dissertation, Pennsylvania State University.

Warren, K. Lee, R.G. and Carroll, M.S. (1992) Timber-dependent communities in crisis: assessing the roles and reactions of rural women. Paper presented at Rural Sociological Society Meetings, Columbus, Ohio, 21 August.

United States Department of Agriculture (1987) *Census of Agriculture,* Washington, DC.

Whatmore, S. (1991) *Farming Women: Gender, Work and Family Enterprise.* London, Macmillan.

CHAPTER 8

Men, Women and Biotechnology: A Feminist 'Care' Ethic in Agricultural Science?

Berit Brandth and Agnes Bolsø[1]

Introduction

Biotechnology raises complex moral issues about the role of human intervention in the world of living beings, and it confronts us with many new questions. Should we allow the release of genetically engineered organisms into the environment? What risks do we run if genetically engineered organisms spread and get out of hand? Should we allow patenting life for profits? What ethical guidelines should we choose when we want to exploit living organisms? In Norway there is an intense public debate about these different aspects of biotechnology. Scientists have tended to emphasise the many great possibilities of biotechnology. Politicians and the general public have been more concerned with negative environmental consequences and food consumers with the health consequences of eating engineered foods. Ethical and religious objections have also been strongly voiced. The farming population is concerned with the ethics involved in pushing the productive capacity of plants and animals, and with the consequences for the future of family farming of the rationalisation process possibly brought about by biotechnology. In general terms, the debate reflects our uncertainty as to whether science and technology are the solution to the world's problems or the cause of them.

Agriculture may be regarded as the key interface between nature and technology. Industrialised farming is heavily dependent on technologies in the shape of mechanical, chemical and biological interventions. As Cochrane

136

(1958, 1979) has pointed out through his theory of 'the technological treadmill', competition between farmers leads to a never-ending adaption of technological innovations, the new biotechnologies being the latest contribution of science. Within agricultural sociology there is a general concern about the environmental consequences of modern farming principles (Goss, 1979; Van Es, 1983). This concern is thematically linked to the feminist critique of science as a project of Western patriarchy (Shiva, 1988). Feminists are criticising the inferior position of women in science and its lack of female perspective. In addition, they are criticising the implications of men's scientific activity. The consequences of masculinist science and technology are depicted as dramatic: it has brought us a deep ecological crisis, symbolised most powerfully by the atom bomb (Merchant, 1980; Easlea, 1983; Shiva, 1988; Hynes, 1989). Modern science, agricultural science included, is a project of Western patriarchy – a project which entails the subjugation of both nature and women, and which therefore cannot be used for emancipatory ends. Thus, it is a feminist project to remake knowledge, Harding claims (Harding, 1986). Science must be created anew in a new social order. Women need sciences and technologies that are *for* women. It is therefore necessary to redesign science to enable it to fabricate knowledge appropriate for women.

In this chapter we are concerned with the relationship between technology and gender in the field of agriculture science. We ask whether men and women differ in their attitudes towards biotechnology as it is being applied in the production of food. In so doing we examine the attitudes of three groups, consumers, farmers and scientists, with different positions in the agro-food chain and thus with different perspectives and relations to this technology.

Feminist critique of science and technology

Feminist scholarship has criticised science and its institutions for being shaped by the interests and concerns of Euro-American middle-class males. In so doing, feminism raises fundamental questions about the nature of truth, objectivity and rationality. The masculine appropriation of knowledge and science in the sixteenth and seventeenth centuries has been analysed by Carolyn Merchant (1980) and Evelyn Fox Keller (1985). In studying the founding texts of Western science, Merchant reconstructs the contexts in which they were made, and shows how Baconian empiricism became a form of power-knowledge important to the mechanistic world view on which capitalism is based. The result has been a natural science preoccupied with power and domination. Nature is seen as something to be controlled and conquered. Today, this is expressed in the quests for the secrets of the atom and the secrets of life itself – the gene.

Merchant's work shows that our conception of nature affects the way we treat it and the way we relate to other species and races (Merchant, 1980), and according to Keller science provides us with models of nature which aim at facilitating specific sorts of interventions (Keller, 1985). Science is a masculine enterprise because it is performed by men and because it perceives nature as if it were a female object. Some of Keller's concern has been with the sexual and reproductive metaphors used in men's scientific discourses, and how these conceptions of knowledge condition what questions can be asked and what aspects of nature can be revealed. What would science have been like if it were constructed on different grounds, she asks? This is also her framework for suggesting alternative constructions of knowledge: she wants to replace the masculinist ideology of science by encouraging scientists to adopt a more interactionist method, by increasing the representation of women, and by urging us to think about what goals we need science to help us achieve.

Also Donna Haraway's concern has been with criticising scientific knowledge as masculine social constructions (Haraway, 1989). By treating the scientific literature of primatology as literary texts, she finds multiple layers of meaning. Such meanings enter the texts independent of the authors' intentions, and as a function of the social and institutional contexts in which the texts are produced. In short, Haraway's interest is to read science to discover the social positions it reflects, and the play of power and politics within the scientific community. On these grounds, her question is how can feminists propose a critique of science and at the same time view science as a source of interest and inspiration? Her answer lies in the image of the cyborg, a creature which figures a mix between the human and the technological. The cyborg does not represent the generic human viewpoint, but embodies the specificity of different locations. Because of this, it is a means to avoid hegemonic forms of thought (Haraway, 1990).

In her book *The Science Question in Feminism* (1986) Harding criticises and rejects the positivist position and practice of science, what she calls 'science as usual'. In developing a feminist epistemology, she examines the argumentation of feminist scientists, and identifies two theories of knowledge which she calls feminist empiricism and feminist standpoint theory. While feminist empiricist research tries to correct 'bad science' by adding knowledge about women's life, standpoint theories tries to correct knowledge by asking questions from the perspective of women's life. Standpoint theories emphasise sexual difference: women's reproductive work and experience of marginality provide them with an understanding of social life that is different from that of men, and it is from this difference position feminist research should begin. Thus, women's greater participation in science can be argued on the basis of equal opportunities, but also on the basis of the qualitatively different values women are expected to bring into the institutions and disciplines of science and technology.

In the next section we will examine some standpoint approaches, associated broadly with 'ecofeminism', which bear on the study of gendered value differences towards technology.

Theories of gender differences in values

Ecofeminism, as it developed in the 1980s, draws together feminist, environmental and women's spirituality movements (Spretnak, 1990); describes women's efforts to save the Earth from ecological disaster; and incorporates a neo-feminist view of women and nature. The feminist tradition from which ecofeminism grew, was that of radical feminism whose analyses of gender inequality sees women as a group dominated by men as a group. This system of domination, called patriarchy, is seen to have derived independently from, but to intersect closely with, capitalism. Fundamental to the development of ecofeminism is the emphasis on the interconnectedness of the domination of women and nature under patriarchal relations. By means of mechanisation, industrialisation and science, patriarchal society is argued to have gained control over life in the form of women, other peoples and nature.

Although ecofeminism is not developed as a coherent social theory (Diamond and Orenstein, 1990), writers often imply and make explicit the equivalence between women and nature, as if women by definition were more life-enhancing and conservationist (Wajcman, 1991). Thus, ecofeminism is criticised for seeing women's values as having a biological basis, and this basis is women's capacity for motherhood. By making reference to 'the way things really are', ecofeminism might fall into the essentialist trap (Quinby, 1990).

Another approach to the understanding of how values may be gendered, is the object-relations theory of Chodorow (1978). This theory, which is often referred to in gender studies of R&D, is a theory about the causes of sexual difference as it describes the mechanisms through which men and women form their relations to the world in different ways. To acquire his masculine identity, the boy has to reject his attachment and identification with the mother. This denial creates less need in the boy to seek acceptance through close relationships with others. He learns to differentiate sharply between himself and others. In the development of girls the continual identification with the mother creates a basis for empathy and otherdirectedness. Thus, masculinity has come to be associated with autonomy, independence and separateness, while femininity is associated with interdependence and empathy – 'a feeling for the organism' which Keller called her study on the female scientist Barbara McClintock (Keller, 1983).

That women's value orientation is different from men's, is empirically observed in many studies. Prokop (1978) finds that because women are socialised to be responsible for society's care functions, they have developed a need-oriented communication. This 'social character' is primarily relational. Sørensen (1984) finds in her studies of workers that men have a 'limited technical rationality' with strong focus on effectivity and productivity. Women have a 'rationality of responsibility' in which the needs and well-being of others are important considerations. Marshall's concepts of 'agency' and 'communion' which is developed to describe coping strategies of men and women in organisations, run along the same lines (Marshall, 1984). 'Agency' emphasises control and independence, 'communion' reciprocity and community.

Together with Chodorow, Carol Gilligan is one of the most cited researchers within the standpoint tradition. In her book 'In a Different Voice', she sets out to correct psychology's misperceptions of women's moral commitments and views of what is important in life (Gilligan, 1982). When women are studied as if they were men, and fail to develop the way men do, the conclusion has been that something must be wrong with women: that they have less rationality and

140

a less developed morality. Instead, Gilligan contends, something must be wrong with theory. In studying how men and women deal with moral dilemmas, she finds as others have done before her, that their moral reasoning is quite different. But, unlike others, she does not take this difference to mean that women have failed to grow to mature adults. The female morality is based on an 'ethic of care', the male on an 'ethic of rights'. One characteristic aspect of the 'ethic of care' is its contextuality: what is right is based on the specific issue in question in its specific context. Another characteristic is the vision of oneself in a web of relationships, where the responsibility towards the others is important. This is contrasted to the 'ethic of rights' where ethical stances are deduced from a hierarchy of general, abstract, context-free principles which are always valid. In short, women see morality as a matter of care, men as a matter of impartial justice.

Caretaking relationships have been important in explaining attributes historically linked with women, also in feminist studies on technology. Standpoint theories are important theories because they insist that values central to women's experience be appreciated, and thus provide directions for social change. However, Gilligan, and standpoint approaches in general, have been criticised for establishing the female rationality as a human norm in replacement of the masculine, and for celebrating sexual difference and the female. Secondly, they have tended to forget 'the down side' of difference. Women's caretaking responsibilities have encouraged disadvantages and a dependency that have carried heavy costs. Thirdly, while Chodorow's and Gilligan's theories can explain difference between men and women and how it is reproduced, it cannot explain difference and variation among women. It is thus accused of homogenisation of women's experiences. The portrayal of women as relational, ignores the complexity of their experience. Women differ from each other in two ways: one is differences resulting from cultural variation, the other is due to hierarchial power relationships between women belonging to different social groups (Harding, 1991).

One of the core issues in the debate on female and male values, is whether existing feminist standpoint theories have a view of women as more unified and undivided than is really the case. The question of whether there is an essential difference between women and men, is part of a wider debate on essentialism in feminist theory. On the one hand there is a great danger that these dichotomies of female and male value orientation might be interpreted as fixed and opposed, and mutually exclusive female and male natures, contending that women are essentially alike and different from men. On the other hand, poststructuralists and postmodernists argue that there is no unity to the category of 'woman', and that analyses based on a dichotomy between 'women' and 'men' suffer from the flaw of essentialism (Segal, 1987; Alcoff, 1988; Fraser and Nicholson, 1988). One issue which has been raised, is that what appears as true female, is only what has been ascribed to women by patriarchy. Authentic and fixed femaleness does not exist. Rather, femaleness is historically and culturally variable, and thus it is created and recreated.

In her book *Whose Science? Whose Knowledge?* Sandra Harding (1991) defends standpoint theories against several different criticisms, also essentialist interpretations. It is the objective position 'from women's lives' that gives standpoint theories legitimacy, not women's biology or women's common experience. To start research from the perspective of the lives of women, also means to start it from the lives of women in oppressed races, classes and cultures. Standpoint approaches can be grounded in differences 'within women' as well as between women and men (Harding, 1991: 180). Knowledge is socially situated. Thus, standpoint theories are neither essentialist nor non-essentialist, she argues. They contain tendencies in several directions; they contain contradictions.

Today, feminists are making concessions to the variety of ways in which to be a woman. Studies of gendering tend to transcend dualism and look for variations both between women, and for feminine and masculine gender traits within individuals. The social construction of femininity (and masculinity) has developed strong themes in the sociology of gender. The dominant cultural idea of what it means to be a woman might neither correspond to most women's personalities, nor to the cultural forms of what, for example, a good female farmer or scientist is. In this paper we deal with culturally specific forms of sex differences in studying women and men having different locations in the agro-food chain, and their attitudes towards agricultural science.

The relationship between values and the production and use of technology is problematic. Today there is a debate about whether 'women matter' – whether there can be a feminine or a 'degendered' science and technology, and what it would look like (Richards and Schuster, 1989; Harding, 1991; Keller, 1991; Sørensen, 1992). Apart from theoretical discourses, little empirical work has been done to explore it.

The ambition of this paper is to investigate this issue within the arena of agricultural science. Our special concern is with women as agricultural scientists, and the question we address is whether there is a different moral attitude towards biotechnology in women than in men. Are the ethical questions concerning the production and use of biotechnology in agriculture more important to women than to men? If so, under what circumstances can we expect to find such differences? As agriculture is a primary arena for investigating relations between technology and nature, the question of whether women matter is particularly important. Will women correct masculinist views of science if given a chance in the production and use of agricultural science?

The data we will use to analyse the question of women's values in relation to biotechnology comes from three different samples. The first one is a national opinion poll done in cooperation with the Market and Media Institute (MMI) in Norway. The survey was done in January 1991, and involved interviews with 1,085 persons, 532 men and 553 women. It contains questions about knowledge of biotechnology, attitude towards genetic engineering and the extent to which the government should control the release of genetically manipulated organisms into the environment, ethical concerns and consumer attitudes towards meat and diary products of biotechnical processes.

The second sample consists of farmers. Data was collected through interview surveys of 525 farms based on the responses of 485 men and 40 women. The same is representative of Norwegian farms and of the farming population with respect to sex and age. The questions asked concern much the same problem areas as the national sample. In addition, there are questions concerning the farmers' situation as producers of food. The material is collected by two colleagues (Almås and Blekesaune, 1989).

The third sample consists of in-depth interviews with 32 scientists within the biotechnical area. They were chosen from lists of researchers working within the biotechnical research programme of the Agricultural Research Council of Norway. Twenty-six men and six women were interviewed. This sample is not representative with regard to sex as the representation of women within this field of research is close to 50 per cent. Each interview lasted from one and a half to three hours. Topics covered were such as career and professional affiliation, type of research, consequences of biotechnical research, ethical and environmental issues, and future prospects for biotechnical R&D. These interviews were done by colleagues at the Centre for Rural Research (Almås, 1991). In addition we have interviewed six women researchers within biotechnology. In these interviews we were especially concerned about women's situation within this discipline of research, and we were interested in possible gender differences.

The groups represented in these samples are different in their relationship to technology. The samples were designed for different purposes. Most of the theory we have referred to is primarily relevant for the question of men and women's different orientations towards R&D. However, when we bring the samples together, it is in order to investigate the circumstances under which sex differences appear. Turning to our data, we ask whether women, more than men, are concerned about the ethical implications of biotechnological research in agriculture. Do women have a different value orientation from men?

Do women have a different moral voice?

Genetic engineering is the most central part of biotechnology. A precondition for genetic engineering is the transfer of genes from one organism to another. If you for ethical reasons are negative towards such transfers, you are negative towards genetic engineering as a whole. Let us first look at attitudes towards the transfer of genes among consumers.

According to Table 8.1, women find genetic engineering less acceptable than men. The differences between women and men (2 per cent vs 8 per cent and 41 per cent vs 33 per cent) are statistically significant at the level of 1 per cent. This difference is confirmed in the answers to questions about the use of more specific biotechniques. Women more than men want to prohibit the release of genetically engineered organisms into the environment. Women more than men will not buy meat or dairy products processed by means of hormones. Women more than men are against the right to patent engineered plants or animals. This sex difference in value orientation is confirmed in similar studies done in the United States (OTA, 1987) and in the European Community (INRA, 1991; Borre, 1989, 1990).

For both women and men in our sample, the ethical reservations decrease

Table 8.1 'By transfering genes, we encroach on the genetic heritage material of plants and animals. How do you consider the ethical aspects?' MMI sample, 1991 (by percentage).

	Women	Men	Total
Ethically acceptable	2	8	5
Ethically doubtful	21	28	25
Ethically unacceptable	41	33	37
Difficult to say/no answer	35	31	34
Sum	101	100	101
N =	553	532	1085

significantly when the levels of education and income increase. The difference between women and men is less obvious in the highest income group. This is not so in the case of education where the gender difference nearly disappears in the highest and the lowest of the four educational groups while it remains significant on the 5 per cent level in the two middle groups.

As a whole, these results may be taken as a confirmation of the feminist critique of science and technology: that women do have a different orientation towards science and technology. Their stronger voice of ethical concerns might be an indication of a more caring rationality.

Men and women of the farming profession

The farmers were asked the same question as above about their ethical attitude to the transfer of genes. The distribution is given in Table 8.2.

Table 8.2 'By transfering genes, we encroach on the genetic heritage material of plants and animals. How do you consider the ethical aspects?' Male and female farmers, 1990 (by percentage).

	Women	Men	Total
Ethically acceptable	3	5	5
Ethically doubtful	30	31	31
Ethically unacceptable	43	46	45
Difficult to say/no answer	25	18	19
Sum	101	100	100
N =	40	485	525

We notice that the farmers find it ethically unacceptable to a larger degree than the total population, 45 per cent vs 37 per cent. We also notice that the difference between women and men is not substantial. Controlling for a diversity of background variables does not change that result.

Agricultural work in Norway, although in the process of industrialisation, still involves a substantial part of caring, as the farmer has the responsibility of giving both animals and plants good conditions of growth. It is possible that men's work with plants, animals, and their conditions for life and growth, entails that men easily adapt a more 'feminine' point of view. Besides, both women and men will share the fear of a further rationalisation of farming, a fact that might promote a joint scepticism against the new biotechnical engineering.

As in the first sample, we also asked questions of the farmers on more specific issues. The farmers are food producers, and some biotechniques will be available in their production in the near future. We listed some of these techniques and asked whether or not the respondent would be willing to use them. Concerning plants there are no gender differences in the inclination to be positive to the use of the techniques. When it comes to animals, however, women are more negative. For plants the assessments made are mostly risk versus benefit, while in the case of animals an element of suffering most certainly must come into consideration. That women are more concerned with this aspect might be an indication of their empathy and rationality of care.

Men and women of the sciences

Turning to the scientists within biotechnical R&D, we have to rely on interviews with a much smaller sample. Analysing this material, we find, naturally speaking, that none of the scientists regardless of their sex is against the transfer of genes. 'To go against the research is stupid. It is the application that must be assessed and stopped', one of them said. Neither do we find any differences between men and women in ethical attitude and concern for the environment. In other words, we find no indication that care-related values are more important in the female assessment of the technological implications. Women scientists are not more critical and disapproving than their male colleagues.

Among these scientists, both men and women are familiar with the arguments in the public debate, and they have opinions on these matters. Some of the women as well as some of the men are negative towards patenting life (but not DNA molecules), and some are negative to the release of genetically engineered micro-organisms and plants into the environment without the strictest control. Most women and most men also find encroaching on genetic heritage material ethically acceptable with micro-organisms and plants, less so with animals, but much less acceptable with humans. They are glad they are not working within human medicine.

Men and women alike express that discovering resistance against disease is a very positive result for humans as well as plants and animals. However, when your results are used to choose among lives, ethical considerations become very delicate. But, as one of the women said: 'I think it is better to arrange it so that only female chickens are born, than to gas all the male chickens as is being done today.' Genetic engineering can also be used to neutralise damaging aspects of environments. As a result, both plants and animals can survive in environments that they cannot endure today. Pigs can be made to tolerate stress and aggression, fish to tolerate acid water. However, 'that fish die is a warning to us that something is the matter with the water. To destroy this alarm-system is wrong', one of the men said. Instead of restoring nature, we adapt to a sick environment by means of technology.

Both women and men as scientists see the potential dangers of biotechnology. They claim, however, that at their research institutions, everything is under control. Researchers are conscientious, and they do good work. Risks are minimal. Both women and men emphasise the positive implications of their research: it will actually improve nature, reduce the need for pesticides, lead to greater production at less cost, and better quality products. In the descriptions they give of their research topics, there is little evidence that women choose subjects of research which imply more care for the natural environment.[2] Thus, a difference in value orientation is not apparent.

Selection and socialisation

As several critics have documented, biology and biotechnology are masculinist in character (Bleier, 1984; Keller, 1985). Yet, this is a field of research in which women and men are equal in numbers. For that reason we would expect feminine values to be apparent to a larger degree in biology than in the more male-dominated natural sciences. Although we do not find any sex differences in values among biotechnical researchers, it would probably be wrong to say that caring values are totally nonexistent in the ethical debate among scientists. They are to some degree brought forward by both men and women. However, we do not know whether men have approached feminine thinking or women men's.

To understand the disappearance of sex differences when we deal with groups of similar backgrounds, we have to consider effects of selection and secondary socialisation. Both women and men in this field of research may be recruited and socialised in ways which eliminate differences in care-related values. The women, for instance, are not restricted to a narrow range of experience primarily from home and family work. They are socialised to a natural science discipline (which is masculinist in character) and an institution of academic culture where the expression of care-related values may be complicated. Perhaps feminine values belong to women's private worlds and cannot be expressed in other locations? Workplace norms might make female scientists less inclined to bring in care-related values that they would use in the private arena. In scientific research emphasis is on objectivity and reason, thus making the expression of political and cultural values illegitimate. Women scientists are not educated with any more critical perspectives about their own discipline than are men.

To survive as researchers women must transcend the cultural stereotype of what is feminine. The need to deny this female-ness has been found to be strong with both women farmers (Brandth, 1993) and researchers (Kvande and Rasmussen, 1990) as they primarily want to be acknowledged as professionals, not as women. Women in biotechnical research are both traditional and non-traditional in their choice of education and occupation. When they choose natural sciences rather than the humanities or social sciences, they are untraditional. When they choose the 'soft' part of the natural sciences (biology/chemistry), and not the 'hard' part (physics/mathematics) they are traditional. They are also traditional when, within biology, they choose the laboratory instead of field research. Women in biotechnical research have avoided stereotypical gender decisions. This might increase the tendency towards sexual conformity in values.

Biotechnical R&D is today being questioned by the world outside the academic community. Therefore, it would be too much to expect that people doing this research would take a position against their own work. Rather, attack from the outside might work to create a stronger sense of community within and also a stronger need to legitimise their work. Another important point is that although the number of women almost equals men, there is great difference in the academic position of men and women. Women are mostly found in junior positions. Striving to be taken seriously by the academic community as good scientists is not the best position from which to mark their distance to its conventions. Besides, the strongest critics might already have left the discipline as did Martha Crouch (1990).

It is, however, important to note that gender differences within biotechnical R&D might be accounted for through other aspects than the ethical assessments. There is still strong reason to believe that biotechnical R&D is gendered in a fundamental way, and that this gendering might appear through working style, preferences, career patterns, language, dominance and control, and family orientation. Moreover, we cannot dismiss the possibility that this technology in the future will confront us with experiences and challenges which will bring forth differences between men and women scientists.

Conclusion and discussion

Initially, we asked whether women are more concerned about the ethical implications of biotechnology in agriculture than men are. This question is grounded both in the feminist critique of masculinist science and technology, and in theories and research on value differences between women and men. As we have seen, the answer is both yes and no. This chapter has shown that the differences between women and men become less substantial as we move from a general sample of consumers of food to samples of specific occupational groups (farmers and scientists). In other words, the theories in which women are described as caring, other-oriented and relational, are not supported in all circumstances. If women have different rationalities from men, they are not always expressed.

The results suggest that women's values are different from men's (as seen primarily among consumers), but also that women are different *from each other* under certain circumstances. That women farmers and scientists to a larger degree express values which are similar to their male counterparts might mean that when women's and men's contexts become more similar, they tend to act more alike. We have pointed to some institutional and occupational effects which illustrate processes by which women and men are socially constructed. We might say that although gender is an important part of what constitutes human identity, its influence is heavily dependent on other cultural institutions and ideas. In other words, situational factors play a critical role in how gender-related characteristics are developed and expressed.

Another question we initially asked, was whether women's different value orientations represent a potential for change. Assuming that the apparent similarity we have found between women and men scientists means that it is the women who have adopted the canons of scientific reasoning and not the men who have been influenced by the rationality of their female colleagues, our results are discouraging. They do not give much reason to believe that women scientists will matter a lot in changing the future of agricultural production. The 'add women and stir' approach is certainly not sufficient. However, the data on which we base our conclusions are limited and we must be careful not to conclude too strongly. We have not examined closely the reception of feminist critiques of science by women scientists on the agricultural arena. The question for most women in science has been how to get access to the institutions of science, not how to challenge it. So, in this chapter, instead of showing how science as a masculine construction is being reconstructed by female values, we have ended up showing how gender is being constructed by science – or to express it in terms of Haraway's cyborg vision: 'It is not clear who makes and who is made in the relation between human and machine' (Haraway, 1990: 219). In any case, women have been fitted to science.

Are there, then, reasons to believe that women as consumers and producers of food in a Western capitalist society will make a difference when it comes to the application of biotechnology in the food system? Will women farmers choose to farm in ways less dependent on technological 'plant improvement' and farm more in accordance with sustainable, feminine principles – natur'e principles according to ecofeminism? When we take into consideration that farming in Norway is a masculine occupation, that only 10 per cent of Norwegian farmers are women and that the dominant farming principles are based on masculinist rationality much like science is, the conclusion is close to what we reached regarding science. The question is actually about what alternatives or options women farmers and scientists have? Will diversity *within* scientific activity and farming be capable of taking care of the critique of biotechnology or will it have to rely on attack from *outside?* Is this the point where consumers of food become important? Science and agriculture are intimately embroiled with the structures of power in industrial society and to alter this, the political project of feminism must ally with other social and political movements.

Notes

1. This chapter is based on a research project conducted by both authors and it was first presented as a paper at the conference: 'Gender, Technology and

Ethics', in Luleå, Sweden. Berit Brandth has been responsible for the theoretical elaborations and the revisions of the paper.
2. We would like to thank the biologist Reidun Aalen for helping us with this part of the analysis.

References

Alcoff, L. (1988) Cultural feminism versus post-structuralism: the identity crisis in feminist theory. *Signs,* 13(3): 405–36.

Almås, R. (1991) *Samfunnsmessige konsekvensar av ny bioteknologi.* Report no. 2. Trondheim, Centre for Rural Research.

Almås, R. and Blekesaune, A. (1989) *Brukarstrategiear 1975–90.* Report no. 3. Trondheim, Centre for Rural Research.

Bleier, R. (1984) *Science and Gender: A Critique of Biology and its Themes on Women.* New York, Pergamon.

Borre, O. (1989) *Befolkningens holdning til genteknologi. Diffusion eller mobilisering.* Report no. 3. København, TeknologiNævnet.

Brandth, B. (1993) Kvinner er ikke lenger hva de var. In Brandth, B. and Verstad, B. (eds) *Kvinneliv i landbruket.* Oslo, Landbruksforlaget.

Chodorow, (1978) *The Reproduction of Mothering.* Berkeley, University of California Press.

Cochrane, W.W. (1958) *Farm Prices: Myth and Reality.* Minneapolis, University of Minnesota Press.

Cochrane, W.W. (1979) *The Development of Industrial Agriculture: A Historical Analysis.* Minneapolis, University of Minnesota Press.

Crouch, M.L. (1990) Debating the responsibilities of plant scientists in the decade of the environment. *The Plant Cell,* 2: 275–77.

Diamond, I. and Orenstein, G.F. (eds) (1990) *Reweaving the World: The Emergence of Ecofeminism.* San Franciso, Sierra Club Books.

Easlea, B. (1983) *Fathering the Unthinkable: Masculinity, Scientists and the Nuclear Arms Race.* London, Pluto Press.

Fraser, N. and Nicholson, L. (1988) Social criticism without philosophy: an encounter between feminism and post-modernism. *Theory, Culture and Society,* 5: 373–94.

Gilligan, C. (1982) *In a Different Voice.* Cambridge, Harvard University Press.

Goss, K.F. (1979) Consequences of diffusion of innovations. *Rural Sociology,* 44: 754–72.

Haraway, D. (1989) *Primate Visions: Gender, Race and Nature in the World of Modern Science.* New York, Routledge.

Haraway, D. (1990) A manifesto for cyborgs: science, technology and socialist feminism in the 1980s. In Nicholson, L. (ed.) *Feminism/Postmodernism.* New York, Routledge.

Harding, S. (1986) *The Science Question in Feminism.* New York, Cornell University Press.

Harding, S. (1991) *Whose Science? Whose Knowledge? Thinking from Women's Lives.* New York, Cornell University Press.

Hynes, H.P. (1989) Biotechnology in agriculture and reproduction: the parallels in public policy. In Hynes, H.P. (ed.) *Reconstructing Babylon. Essays on Women and Technology*. London, Earthscan Publications.

INRA, Eurobarometer 35, 1 (1991) *Biotechnology*. Directorate – General Science, Research, Development CUBE – Biotechnology Unit.

Keller, E.F. (1983) *A Feeling for the Organism*. San Franscisco, Witt Freeman.

Keller, E.F. (1985) *Reflections on Gender and Science*. New Haven, Yale University Press.

Keller, E.F. (1991) Spørsmålet om kjønn i vitenskapelig arbeid (Issues of sex and gender in the pursuit of science). *Nytt om kvinneforskning*, 1: 16–22.

Kvande, E. and Rasmussen, B. (1990) *Nye kvinneliv. Kvinner i menns organisasjoner*. Oslo, Ad Notam.

Marshall, J. (1984) *Women Managers – Travellers in a Male World*. Chichester, Wiley.

Merchant, C. (1980) *The Death of Nature: Women, Ecology and the Scientific Revolution*. London, Wildwood House.

Office of Technology Assessment (OTA) (1987) *New Developments in Biotechnology*. Background Paper no. 2. Public Perceptions of Biotechnology.

Plant, J. (ed.) (1989) *Healing the Wounds: The Promise of Ecofeminism*. Philadelphia, New Society Publishers.

Prokop, U. (1978) *Kvinnelig livssammenheng*. Kongerslev, GMT.

Quinby, L. (1990) Ecofeminism and the politics of resistance. In Diamond, I. and Orenstein, G.F. (eds) *Reweaving the World: The Emergence of Ecofeminism*. San Francisco, Sierra Club Books.

Richards, E. and Schuster, J. (1989) The feminine method as myth and accounting resource: a challenge to gender studies and social studies of science. *Social Studies of Science*, 19: 697–720.

Segal, L. (1987) *Is the Future Female? Troubled Thoughts on Contemporary Feminism*. London, Virago Press.

Shiva, V. (1988) *Staying Alive: Women, Ecology and Development*. New Delhi, Zed Books Ltd.

Sørensen, B.Aa. (1984) The organisational women and the trojan-horse effect. In Holter, H. (ed.) *Patriarchy in a Welfare Society*. Oslo, Universitetsforlaget.

Sørensen, K.H. (1992) Towards a feminised technology? Gendered values in the construction of technology. *Social Studies of Science*, 22(1): 5–31.

Spretnak, C. (1990) Ecofeminism: our roots and flowering. In Diamond, I. and Orenstein, G.F. (eds) *Reweaving the World: The Emergence of Ecofeminism*. San Francisco, Sierra Club Books.

Van Es, J.C. (1983) The adoption/diffusion tradition applied to resource conservation: inappropriate use of existing knowledge. *The Rural Sociologist*, 3: 76–82.

Wajcman, J. (1991) *Feminism Confronts Technology*. Cambridge, Polity Press.

For Product Safety Concerns and Information please contact our EU
representative GPSR@taylorandfrancis.com
Taylor & Francis Verlag GmbH, Kaufingerstraße 24, 80331 München, Germany

www.ingramcontent.com/pod-product-compliance
Lightning Source LLC
Chambersburg PA
CBHW062037270326
41929CB00014B/2455

9 781032 497792